Hannah Ferguson is the co-founder and Chief Executive Officer of Cheek Media Co, an independent Australian news commentary platform providing informed, progressive opinions on subjects that sit at the intersection of feminist, social and political issues. Hannah is also the host of news and pop culture podcast *Big Small Talk*. Hannah has a Bachelor of Laws (Honours) and a Master of Publishing, Editing and Writing from the University of Queensland, and is the bestselling author of *Bite Back*, published by Affirm Press in 2023.

PRAISE FOR TABOO

Hannah Ferguson is one of the most reliable, educated and qualified voices for young women in Australia. I'd read anything she writes. *Taboo* arms readers with the knowledge and language to question the status quo and, in turn, gives them the tools to make impactful change in their everyday lives.
– Abbie Chatfield

Ferociously bright, fearless and funny – Hannah Ferguson is the voice we all need to shatter taboos and guide us towards a new truth.
– Elizabeth Day

Taboo is an instant classic. Hannah Ferguson's ability to bring humanity to every polarising conversation she contributes to is what sets her, and this book, apart. As political discourse becomes more and more fragmented, disrespectful and dogged, Hannah ploughs a new path. Her work is open, honest and examined, with a conviction in her beliefs that never borders on dogma. It's a pleasure to watch her think, and it's just as much a pleasure to read it, too. Everyone – yourself, your mum, your partner and your dog – needs to read this book!
– Lucinda Price, aka Froomes

A confronting and cathartic exploration of our most intimate experiences, *Taboo* is another relatable and revolutionary read from one of Australia's most important voices.
– Bridget Hustwaite

Taboo is incredible. It shines light into every dark corner, every shame filled spiral, every curious whisper and secret you've ever held close. The kind of thing you want to make sure everyone from your best friend to your boss to that one uncle we all have reads. It's fearless and true, astonishingly honest and poignant, searingly relatable in its specificity. Ferguson tells the kind of tales that will make you laugh out loud, make your brain explode from thinking in a new way and make your heart ache, possibly all in the same sentence.
– Hannah Diviney

For Lilli and Hayley

and all of our younger selves

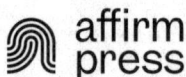

affirm press

First published by Affirm Press in 2024
Bunurong/Boon Wurrung Country
28 Thistlethwaite Street
South Melbourne VIC 3205
affirmpress.com.au

10 9 8 7 6 5 4 3 2 1

Text copyright © Hannah Ferguson, 2024
Illustrations copyright © Samuel Leighton-Dore, 2024

Affirm Press is located on the unceded land of the Bunurong/Boon Wurrung peoples
of the Kulin Nation. Affirm Press pays respect to their Elders past and present.

A catalogue record for this
book is available from the
National Library of Australia

ISBN: 9781923046634 (paperback)

Cover design by Alissa Dinallo © Affirm Press
Typeset in 12/19 pt Minion Pro by Post Pre-press Group, Brisbane
Proudly printed and bound in Australia by Opus Printing Group

MIX
Paper | Supporting
responsible forestry
FSC® C001695

Taboo

Hannah Ferguson

affirm
press

Taboo contains material that may be distressing for some readers. These subjects range from sexual and domestic violence to disordered eating. Please read with care for yourself first and seek professional support if this content raises concerns for you.

Some details have been changed to protect the privacy of individuals referenced in *Taboo*.

contents

taboo: noun

A social ban or avoidance of a subject based on a community's belief that it is repulsive, offensive, sacred or exclusively for enjoyment and discussion by certain people. It is a pressure point, a prescription for how to behave in public. Taboos regulate our behaviour and ensure we do not cross the boundaries of social custom determined by those in power, to benefit them. Anyone who dares invoke it creates a powerful, often negative, reaction in those around them.

taboo: reality

Any conversation that frays the fabric of patriarchy. A subject clouded in stigma that serves systems and institutions of power. The function of a taboo is to silence. It ensures you do not question the status quo. It requires you to remain in discomfort, for the continued comfort of men. It enforces the boundaries of shame, who feels it and why. Taboo is a silencer of truth, and therefore accountability. Taboo is a locked door, with change sitting on the other side. Subjects are not taboo; experiences that challenge the power structures upheld by straight, white, cisgender, able-bodied men are.

––––––––

my taboo opinions

1. Your romantic partner isn't your best friend: that undermines the meaning and purpose of friendship.

2. Sex is a mental act more than a physical one.

3. Motherhood is taught as a calling, but it is foremost hard work.

4. Getting botox isn't a feminist act.

5. Gossip is a valuable component of social connection.

6. Women are most celebrated for 'milestones' that limit our independence. The social markers for heterosexual female success are the extent to which we centre men and children, not ourselves.

7. We live in a culture obsessed with wellness, and yet we have never been more sick.

8. Women proposing to men is not progressive or subversive, it is just women taking on the one thing men are expected to plan, execute and be vulnerable in during romantic relationships.

9. Our obsession with anti-ageing insults the beauty of our mothers and grandmothers.

10. We need to think less about ourselves; our fixation on our appearances is the patriarchy winning.

———

11. In a heteronormative society where women have had our pleasure suppressed and it has been normalised to 'tolerate' sex with men, we must be intentional about seeking freedom in our sexuality, or we risk never truly finding it.

12. Hating yourself is a form of internalised misogyny to be unlearned.

13. Women work more hours than men; men have simply built an economic system that only values men's contributions.

14. Taboos are a mechanism used to make women feel shame about their bodies, stories and experiences.

———

introduction

The first time I heard anyone talk about female masturbation was when I was fifteen. Yes, that is the first sentence of this book. I was at a birthday party, and the year was 2014. I was in grade ten and a group of girls in my year went for lunch at the Hog's Breath Cafe in town. We dressed up to take heavily filtered sepia-toned Instagram photos over the chocolate cake topped with sparklers. Sixteen of them. The Snapchat puppy dog filter was in, and Taylor Swift was about to release *1989*, the album that would catapult her to an entirely new tier of superstardom. Hog's Breath was a staple birthday venue in our regional New South Wales town, Orange. I try to black out most of those years of my life, but two things I will never forget are (1) this story and (2) the $12.50 chicken caesar wraps and curly fries meal deal during the two-hour lunch session.

On this particular rainy Saturday, twelve of us piled

around one of the long wooden tables towards the front of the restaurant, which was decorated in what I would describe as a shed-chic aesthetic. Pinterest has never seen anything like it. After an hour and a half of debating which of our teachers was the creepiest, sharing screenshots of messages from boys we liked and checking who was listed as the top three best friends on every person's Snapchat, we landed on the topic of masturbation. I had never done it, and I had never talked about it before. I remember looking down at my ankle boots, gold-zippered and scuffed, not wanting to make eye contact with any of the giggling friends who were offering up their thoughts in hushed voices. My cheeks began to burn as I dipped a chip in aioli, careful to chew for as long as I could and avoid eyes assessing my response. It was the first time in my life I had shut the fuck up. These girls were some of my closest friends. We knew boys in our grade did it, because they talked about it. They shared porn videos and blasted moaning noises through their phones and couldn't make it through even one of our health and physical education lessons without being sent out, when all we were instructed to do was complete a worksheet matching contraceptives to their definitions. Boys would laugh or mock any mention of pads and tampons, but some encouraged each other to circulate nude images they had been sent by a girl they were talking to, or on one occasion a video that was non-consensually taken of their girlfriend performing a blowjob. These images made the girl 'slutty' in the eyes of many students and teachers. The boys who shared them were slapped on the wrist. Then the police were brought in to give a legal talk and that was that. I'm sure this was the cycle at many schools.

I wish I was about to describe a defining moment in friendship, one where girls who went to a conservative religious school that controlled every element of our uniform – from mandating knee-high socks, to teachers conducting random makeup-wipe swipes throughout the day, to compulsory calf-length skirts and attempting a ban on wearing hair ties on our wrists – had an open conversation about pleasure and our bodies. If I'd had the emotional maturity, this could have pivoted my entire perception of my body and my sexual understanding. But, of course, that isn't what happened. Instead at least 70 per cent of the party attendants ostracised the two girls who had disclosed their experiences of masturbation to us. I honestly can't remember if we decided to ostracise them in the moment, or privately afterwards. Regardless, we judged them and shamed them; I know I did. I nervously giggled that I would NEVER do that. Picking up the remnants of my wrap, shoving it into my face, I texted my mum that I would be ready to go in fifteen.

I went home and thought about the conversation for weeks. It prompted me to try masturbating for the first time. I learned more about my body in those weeks than in the years of lacklustre, uncomfortable sex ed my school offered; but those learnings didn't stop me from telling my other friends, who hadn't been invited to Hog's Breath, about the conversation. I was not just shaming the two girls who had told me it was normal to want to feel pleasure; I was imposing that same stigma on others by spreading a lie I told myself day in day out: that masturbation was not normal. This is one of those stories that keeps me up at night, sitting with the realisation that the child in me hurt other children who were actually just so far ahead of me. The openness of those girls on that day was something I can still learn and benefit from even now. Children can be so mean. Mostly, we learn it from adults.

The truth about high school is that every person wants to be the cool one having sex, the 'experienced' and 'awakened' person who's started early. They were the experts in something I couldn't even fathom. As I walked my colour-coordinated binders to school, desperate to be just like them, to know the secrets they knew, I also remember thinking there was something boy-obsessed about it, something precious and clean that they had ruined. I felt inferior to them, and my internalised misogyny worked in overdrive to make me superior once more.

At this birthday party, which should have been a safe space for friends to share, we were so afraid to admit that we'd humped a pillow, listened to Michael Bublé on a plane (this was my sexual awakening at the age of nine – I cried because I was scared of that tingly feeling I didn't understand), or used the tap in the bath to feel something.

For most of us at the table, instead of opening ourselves up to a new idea, our fear operated as a strong all-encompassing defence mechanism. My nervous system was activated, and I felt myself shut down. Heart racing, conversation closing. Collectively, we attempted to impose a standard on the girls who were unencumbered by this taboo. Our fear tried to work others into submission.

Shame is an infection that the most insecure, the fearful, are all too desperate to share. Sometimes I wonder how having these conversations with my friends earlier could have helped me. I wonder how the girls who were brave enough to share felt after that moment. I reflect on all the shame-fuelled things I may have said that I cannot recall, of all the people I hurt when I didn't know better than to shame girls and hate myself. In those moments my friends were not heard, seen or known. They were made to feel perverse, slutty, horny. These are the worst things women can be told they are.

Now, I look back and wish I got to be one of the girls who touched themselves. What would it mean for me now if I had been open and able to explore, feel and pleasure myself from a younger age? I do not know these women any more, but I hope it set them up to learn more about their own sexuality. I hope they will not look at me now and despise my current openness. It would be fair if they did. The fact is: they helped me progress at, perhaps, a significant cost to themselves.

A few years later, when I was twenty-one, I started to engage in a pattern of getting really drunk and talking to everyone at parties and in club toilets about vibrators. I was an absolute menace. I should have printed pamphlets and business cards because, for a period of time, it was what I became known for. Watch out for Three-Drink Ferg: you'll have a clit-sucking orgasm machine added to your cart in less than sixty seconds. I didn't discriminate, either; men would have their card tapped for a partner's gift and women would be exploring what to add to their collections in equal measure. It was like a Tupperware party no one had asked to attend. People mocked me and said that I should have been given an affiliate discount code, so succinct and consistent was my pitch. It wasn't just because I was more compelling than a shopping channel infomercial presenter trying to sell you a bedazzled casket before 8am. I think the only time I witnessed women and men having open conversations about pleasure was when alcohol was involved.

But I hadn't escaped my inner fifteen-year-old self entirely. I would wake the next day and be so ashamed of myself that I would regularly not leave my bed until 7 or 8pm. I would sit down in the shower and call myself a pervert. I would tell myself I was disgusting. It was genuinely that bad for at least two years. I used alcohol consumption as a way to let go of control. As an intense, highly strung eldest child who dedicated much of her life to being impressive on paper and receiving applause, drinking was a way to my authentic self without the limitations of shame and fear. My bodily response when the effects wore off was the chemical restoration of those anxieties: it was shame in overdrive. I had ripped off the boundaries of a taboo like a bandaid, and when I came to, the discomfort tripled.

I was trying desperately to be vulnerable, but without doing it authentically. I was being forcibly, overly open without boundaries, not respecting myself enough to do so unless I was inebriated. I was having conversations when other people were drunk and who may not have wanted to hear about the thirteen settings the palm vibrator on my bookshelf had.

The positives of my openness were clear, in spite of this. Now I think more kindly about what I actually did: get groups of women to talk about and invest in their own sexual pleasure. I ultilised the comfort and safety and permission of lowered inhibitions to share what I had learned in my own life: that pleasure can change your relationship with your body, with sex and with yourself. I wanted to tell my friends, but I just couldn't do it without getting drunk.

These conversations led to people I love feeling safe to disclose their abortions for the first time. The men in my life were able to ask how to incorporate vibrators into their partnered sex lives. I hated myself for what I said and did, yet the response I was getting showed me I needed to do this sober – that sex and pleasure were things people wanted to talk about, and that they were excited to have a space where they could explore the subjects free from judgement.

Fast forward four years and I've made my own vibrator.

Taboo

I have helped develop an accessible sex toy and a set of intimacy cards for destigmatising conversations between sexual partners, and to use during solo pleasure. I went from denying, to talking, to owning, to promoting, to reviewing, to *producing* a product. It took me seven years to go from shaming someone to feeling shame to destigmatising it. I don't want people to have to go through this process. I want women to be born into comfort. My sister, who is seven years younger than me, got her first vibrator before she was even the same age as me when I attended that fateful birthday lunch at the elegant Hog's Breath. She called me to do an unboxing, holding it up to the speaker so I could listen to the different settings. That is the disintegration of taboo.

Shame is a lie I tell myself, one I believe. That I am bad. That I am unworthy of love. That a thought or a behaviour or a belief or an action makes me fundamentally wrong. When we fail to challenge these beliefs, we submit to a rulebook written for us but not for our benefit.

Writing *this* book, I hope, will allow me to invalidate the lies I have believed about my body, my relationships and my work to date. I hope that you too identify the narratives you tell the world each and every day and begin rewriting them as needed. I want to explore what the world could be like for women if we didn't feel smothered by the hand of patriarchy – if we were not so worn down by opposition that we became agreeable and began to believe in our own inferiority.

What I'm describing is exhausting: fighting the language

and the shame and the undermining at every turn. A taboo is, in many ways, a failed connection. It is rejecting a bid for conversation because of discomfort. Every time you say how you feel, you are dismantling a stigma that's working to dehumanise you. I'm inviting you instead to sit in discomfort and consider the small ways we, as women, have allowed ourselves to be shamed out of joy and honesty. Because *we are the taboo*. Our experience is what is being regulated. According to patriarchy, stating the problem makes you the problem. I have built a career from explaining to people how the media utilises language to distort our understanding of politics, law and power. But how has the language of womanhood, and the absence of it, defined and slowed the fight for equality?

✖

I am exhausted by women's secrecy around our bodily functions, yet I remain so ashamed of so many parts of myself. Knowing something intellectually does not equate to being emotionally able to process it. I still have an eating disorder. I remain uncomfortable talking about money and am still struggling to value myself outside work. I am tired of being called 'antimen' for telling women they deserve better than a boyfriend who cannot find the bread in the pantry or make a booking for a date but expects a blowjob every second day. I want to know why it's acceptable that my uncle wished my partner luck and informed him I was 'a big handful' the first time they met. I will probe my grandfather for asking me if I'm having children, but not checking whether it's in my brother's plans. Pornography taught me how to scream, how to fake an orgasm but not how to ask for consent, use protection or experience pleasure. I feel more shame for responding 'That's not okay,' at the dinner table than my family member does for saying women accusing men of rape just 'regret' sex the day after.

But we know it isn't just men. Just as often it is women who have made me feel small. It is me who has beaten me down most. I wonder how many experiences of their own shame, silencing, objectification and belittling it takes for women to turn on each other. At what point did it become easier for some mothers and grandmothers and aunties and colleagues to decide, consciously or not, to help patriarchy flatten our womanhood, instead of leaning further into it? How would I feel about myself, my body and my brain if the world valued women? What would my life look like if the world was able to hold space for women's experiences and worked to accommodate instead of control them?

The existence of taboos has allowed language to control us. Words are a powerful stimulus: they can increase our tolerance for discomfort or create a nuclear explosion at a house party. Taboos have silenced women's experiences, stories and knowledge-sharing. This book explores some of the experiences I've had that I believed at the time were entirely my own. I have been terrified that they made me less of a woman, a failed feminist and alone in my body and mind. By sharing them, I rid them of the power to isolate me.

Is sex taboo? Because presidents have no trouble boasting about grabbing women by the pussy. Men are more than happy to discuss their body counts, to talk about fucking and nailing and banging and finishing. Taboo enters the chat when clitoral stimulation, strap-ons, scissoring, period sex and vibrators do.

Money, I'll argue, isn't actually taboo, either. When we say money is an 'off-limits' subject, we are not expecting male entrepreneurs to feel uncomfortable dishing their salaries, their investment portfolios or mansplaining how the economy works. Male wealth is allowed to be aspirational. Women should thrive in silence, because our 'nice things' are considered frivolous and unnecessary. We are not allowed to earn large amounts of money, which threatens men who believe they are meant to be the 'breadwinners'. Nor are we to have money and be visibly wealthy, or to ask for more of it confidently in professional settings (that's before we even touch on cascading taboos, like the experience of women negotiating child support with men).

Is religion taboo? Or is institutional child sexual abuse committed by male clergy a concealed epidemic? Are we uncomfortable with death? Or are we a patriarchal society lacking the emotional intelligence and mental-health infrastructure to help people communicate and process their grief?

These are just some of the conversations we rarely have, and which I believe we must approach now. And yes, a twenty-five-year-old writing a book about navigating modern womanhood sounds unexpected. But is it ridiculous that a young person would have things to say about a wellness culture that has tried to convince her she feels bad all the time because she has high cortisol levels, not because the world around her is burning? Is it absurd that a young woman who has amassed a following of more than 130,000 people would be confident enough to explore conversations around bodies, dating culture and the future of women's labour? Could it be just a fantasy that people would want to buy a book whose author does not claim to have the answers but wants to provoke the questions we are not asking about motherhood, contraception, 'having it all' and female friendship? I have never had the solutions, but I have the stark naivety – scratch that – *bravery* to start the conversations no one feels ready to have.

I do not feel equipped to talk about the decision to become a parent, and I have no clue what going through menopause is like. I am not pretending to know, but there's a reason I do not. While our conversational capacity around women's health and reproductive experiences has grown significantly, patriarchy still does not want us to access this information at an early age, if ever. Many women continue to suffer in silence, to minimise their pain and to seek information only once they are in the throes of pregnancy, menopause, infertility, polycystic ovary syndrome and more. Women's health is not an area of proactive education, but of post-diagnosis confusion and obsession.

Introduction

As a generation Z woman, the world often tells me what I am before I am able to define it myself. It is a tale as old as time. Radical. Different. Unappreciative. Too woke. Subversive. These words splinter us from other women not only through the Murdoch media, but in conversations I've had with millennial, generation X and baby boomer people in my life. In all likelihood, the women reading this who are not part of my demographic will have made assumptions and applied stereotypes to us, as we have to them. The headlines and social media trends categorising me and my fellow gen Zs are designed to ostracise and alienate us from the experiences of those before, to ensure the waves of feminism never feel capable of crashing together to shore. While my experiences are innately my own, I hope to offer perspectives that have the energy and the potential to branch into new territory of questions, privileges and niches that still remain somewhat uncharted, a future that has been supported by the women who came before us.

You may not agree with me, but I'll try my best to show you how I've ended up on the path I currently walk. If you wince at my age, if you cringe at my thought processes and judgements with the insight of being further into your life than me – I understand. But I want to ask why things had to be so hard for you. I want to ask on behalf of my generation how we ensure that does not continue. Sometimes, naivety is a key ingredient of change. My lack of understanding says: that does not make sense. It shouldn't have been that way for you, and I do not want it to be that way for me. I shouldn't have to 'tolerate' or 'endure' sex with my partner. I do not need to spend in excess of $50,000 on a wedding to 'legitimise' my relationship. Why is having children the default? And are we capable of talking openly and honestly about the roads we regret not taking?

I hope this book is one giant fucking problem for men, for patriarchy and for the continued existence of taboos. I want you to be more difficult, more inconvenient and more uncomfortable than before you read it. I want you to challenge the status quo and break the uncomfortable silence you've been sitting in. In a review of Greta Gerwig's billion-dollar feminist film, *Barbie*, Dr Simon Longstaff narrows in on the central message of the film that so many missed:

> How many of us consciously embrace our humanity – and all of the implications of doing so? How many of us wonder about what it takes to become fully human? Gerwig implies that far fewer of us do so than we might hope … Instead, too many of us live the life of the dolls – no matter what world we live in. We are content to exist within the confines of a box; to not think or feel too deeply, to not have our lives become more complicated as when happens when the rules and conventions – the morality – of the crowd is called into question by our own wondering.

Introduction

In this book I'm not shaming women or hating men: I'm asking you to explore what could exist if we fight to step outside of the box's confines. I do not want to be prescriptive: I want to invite wonder.

It is taboo for women to say we do not want to have casual sex. It is taboo to enjoy casual sex without strings or emotions. It is taboo to exist in your body comfortably, without positive or negative feelings about it. It is taboo to choose something for yourself without consulting, seeking advice from or considering others. It is taboo to succeed. To choose not to have children. To not want to get blind drunk every Saturday night because you'd prefer to lie on the couch with a warm drink and your favourite socks on. To ask for more. To like yourself and not question it. It is taboo to want to talk about your experience of being a woman.

These are the conversations we've missed.

1
body

what i would tell my fifteen-year-old self about her body

1. Do not go on the pill just to manage acne: it is going to do damage in the process of clearing your skin.

2. You are memorable because of your height. It intimidates exactly the kind of man you want to intimidate. Stop hunching. You are unforgettable.

3. Pee after sex straight away, every single time.

4. You will look back on photos from six months ago and think you were 'so much prettier then'. You will do this every six months for all of eternity if you do not start believing that you are beautiful as you are now.

5. Preventative botox isn't a thing, so stop opening your wallet to an industry that hates you.

6. If a doctor isn't listening to you, go to another one.

7. Do not focus on making physical changes to yourself: focus on your mental health to help you embrace your physical self as it is.

8. Do not focus on how your body looks during sex: focus on how your body feels during sex.

9. Track your menstrual cycle: it helps make sense of EVERYTHING.

10. Do not put soap inside your vagina: it cleans itself.

11. You queef in specific sex positions and it is really funny, not disgusting.

12. Pain during sex isn't normal. I wish we'd spoken to a health professional much earlier than we did.

13. Stop straightening your hair so much: it is damaging, and it is not you.

14. You have generalised anxiety disorder which isn't diagnosed for another six years, though you thought you were *just* a stressed and efficient parentified eldest child who placed her value in productivity. Talk to someone about this earlier.

15. It isn't normal to feel like you are going to get in trouble all the time: your nervous system is in overdrive.

16. Clean your belly button, babe.

17. Your sister is watching you so be careful how you talk about yourself.

18. Unfortunately, exercise, routine, sleep and good nutrition do make you feel your best.

19. You drink to escape yourself and to feel comfortable having sex. It will always make you feel worse.

20. Do not spend a mortgage on a skincare routine, but wear sunscreen every day.

taboo 1:

✗

Beauty, Body Image and the Pursuit of Eternal Youth

I am the right amount of pretty, thin and privileged to be tolerated. I think about this a lot as someone in a public-facing job. Much of my success is due to the fact that I am white, tall and educated. My future success closely depends on my ability to ensure I am the right balance of funny and intelligent, attractive but not too attractive. I am safe as the 'girl next door'. Not wealthy, but also not living in poverty, which invites a distinct kind of judgement and stereotyping. Be likeable.

Taboo

Be thin, but don't flaunt it. Be pretty, just enough. As a young woman existing on the internet, my choice of what not to post is more important than what I do share. I make conscious choices every time I post to ensure I am more often barefaced and pimply than made over and styled. For the first year or two of Cheek, this was simply accidental. It was and is my authentic approach. But as my following, and the scrutiny that comes with that, has grown, so has my strategy and calculation regarding how I appear, when I disappear and why. Sometimes, it's plain exhaustion. Mostly, it's to manage oversaturation, so I don't become annoying or unlikable. If I look hot or try hard to look pretty, am I perceived as detaching from the mission I actively fight for? I am purposeful with how I dress, because I know what accompanies the social branding of being sexualised.

Do I care about all of this too much? Yes, of course, and that's patriarchal in nature. But if I don't consider the responsibility I hold, it may also be the thing that isolates the people who once connected with me. Existing as a woman, and particularly as a feminist woman, is precarious. This is my experience, but I believe it is also how we have been trained to perform by social media. Every person with an Instagram account feels compelled to present their personality, their appearance, their body, their decisions, their views and their lifestyle in a way that has a positive impact on those who follow them. Whether those followers actually value the poster's opinion or are even current friends is a moot point. Consciously or not, we understand social media as a tool for self-expression and representation. In Elle Hunt's piece 'Everyone's so intolerant online. Am I right to stay silent?' she discusses Africa Brooke's book, *The Third Perspective*.

> In *The Third Perspective*, Brooke sets out how our innate desire to belong to 'the in-group' combines with the structural design of online platforms to perpetuate pile-ons. They are dehumanising by nature, leading you to think of yourself as an 'employee of Instagram', obliged to contribute your thoughts, opinions and anger – and to manage others you see as letting the side down. Opting out altogether is not always possible, with people increasingly obliged to maintain digital presences for their work and relationships.

Every person's social media presence is a subconscious marketing exercise. With every post, every like, every comment, every share and every caption we are curating a persona of ourselves that feels safe to share. We cultivate likeability. We carefully consider how we announce pregnancies, engagements, birthday parties and property purchases, and even the order of images in a carousel post to achieve the perfect balance of relatable and aspirational. When I see these highly constructed posts, I hear the echo of our own moral perfectionism: 'I am successful by the metrics others have set for me.' How we choose to highlight achievement, beauty and lifestyle is a measure of our algorithms; our social circles have the power to define what we feel is worthy of promotion. For some people, the commodity of grid space is more important than the actual feeling of the milestone itself. We are less concerned with showing our actual travel experience than with proving to others that we are fashionable, aesthetic and cultured. Appearances are more important than our actual lives. We want to be seen as thin, pretty and happy – whether we actually are the last part or not is beside the point. We care less about being seen, and more about being understood as the person we aspire to be. Thin, informed, fun, privileged – but just the right amount. We want to be pretty and comfortable. We want to be liked more than we want to be understood.

This isn't just a factor in our algorithms; we know pretty privilege impacts our lifelong earnings and success within workplaces, social circles and beyond. Astrid Hopfensitz, a professor in organisational behaviour at EM Lyon Business School, confirmed this in her piece for *The Conversation*, '"Pretty privilege": attractive people considered more trustworthy, research confirms'. Hopfensitz describes the economic advantage gained by meeting social beauty standards thus:

> Numerous studies have shown that attractive individuals benefit from a beauty bonus and earn higher salaries on average. Certain high-paying professions are built around beauty (such as show business) but

what is more surprising is that for almost any kind of employment, beauty can lead to a positive halo effect. Beautiful individuals are consistently expected to be more intelligent and thought to be better leaders, which influences career trajectories and opportunities.

It is thought individuals perceived as beautiful are also more likely to benefit from people's trust, which makes it easier for them to get promoted or to strike business deals. The idea is that individuals who look better are thought to be healthier or/and to have had more positive social interactions in their past, which might influence their trustworthiness.

We know that pretty privilege exists, but we also know that the cost over a lifetime that women spend on their appearance adds up to approximately US$225,000. I read this 2017 research in an opinion piece by the founder of independent news source *Zee Feed*, Crystal Andrews – 'The pursuit of beauty: a high price for faux-empowerment':

Under the patriarchy, conformity to the beauty standard is safety. The pretty privilege girlies don't want you to know this, but the further you are from The Beauty Standard the worse everyone will treat you – the system and the individuals within it. Less opportunities, more harassment; less consideration, more violence. The halo effect of attractiveness is well-documented.

This is the sticking point where discussions about feminism in beauty always get tripped up. Who am I to denounce other womens' defense mechanisms from patriarchy and white supremacy? Camouflage makes you less of a target, sharpening the knife makes it hurt a little less. If decorating your cage brings a morsel of joy even as it dissolves your own feathers, then you might as well do it – we're not getting out of the cages either way. Unadorned bars are not freedom.

Every time we judge another woman, every time we alter ourselves, every time we expect women to conform to an impossible standard in a new and fucked way, we permit men to do the same. This system is driven by capitalism and the beauty companies that have commodified our self-hatred, but at what point do we as 'victims' of patriarchy also become perpetrators who maintain and enforce it? We see ageing as a failure, not a privilege. We degrade ourselves and other women into conforming to a system that hates us. At what point must we reckon with the conditions and truly examine and criticise ourselves and each other for participating in and aspiring to the beauty standards that we pursue to please patriarchy? No matter how you look, you will still be hurt by this system. Pretty privilege gives us the illusion that we control the extent, nature and timing of its infliction.

In March 2024, LEGO Group released a global study that

examined the way our language bias impacts the creativity of girls. Surveying over 61,500 parents and children aged five to twelve years old across thirty-six countries, the results showed that society is around seven times more likely to attribute terms like 'sweet', 'pretty', 'cute' and 'beautiful' exclusively to girls, while terms such as 'brave', 'cool', 'genius' and 'innovative' are twice as likely to be attributed exclusively to boys. The research also revealed over half of children believe adults listen more to boys' creative ideas than to girls'.

From a young age, we teach girls that their minds are inferior. Women are ornaments to be observed, not creators to be respected. The way this manifests over time can be seen in everyday interactions; we learn to measure ourselves against other girls' appearances, and our ability to perform femininity for the parents who impose the gendered system they have also grown up in on us. It is no wonder that we continue to prod, poke and alter ourselves when the prejudice of our world told us we were more valuable as the art than as the artist.

This teaching is fundamentally flawed, and we all know it. The reality is, we will age and we will never be fulfilled fighting to remain the object of society's affection and admiration. The meanest trick of all is, you never were. The language of the beauty industry monetises a fight we will never win. No matter how thin, pretty or close to the beauty standard we are: we feel it is always out of reach. The image of 'the perfect woman' is always in flux, but one thing remains stable: in Western culture, white, thin and symmetrical has always been the brief. I don't believe any woman has ever felt that she truly has 'reached' the beauty standard, but it is vital to remember that many women have been wholly excluded from it. As a woman holding many privileges, I can look at the blueprint and identify where I'm failing. But black women, transgender women, disabled women, fat women, Asian women and so many others know the model for how to be doesn't include them. I may feel 'less than', but that is not comparable to being entirely excluded from the Western world's parameters for beauty. Exclusion and denigration exist on a spectrum: these conversations require us to identify the problem, but also our various roles within the privileged group and how we benefit from them. I don't look like a poster girl, but she represents many of the privileges I have. Our fixation must be accompanied by awareness.

I want us to ask ourselves what it could feel like to take this focus, this obsession with all the ways we aren't enough – and channel it into something constructive. What if we could regain the creativity of our five-year-old selves? Could we again be the artist instead of the object? What could we create if we weren't so occupied by all the ways we don't measure up? When we compare ourselves to every woman we pass, we are also undermining *their* capacity to be creators. As I said earlier, self-hatred is internalised misogyny. If we do not unpack it, we will pass it on to all our children. Bridging the gap between our feminism and our treatment of ourselves might seem like the last thing to focus on, but it is the most important work we will do. If we examine and heal our thoughts, actions and behaviours regarding and towards ourselves and other women, we will raise a generation of feminist children who see themselves as we see them: loved.

Three months ago while I was FaceTiming my eighteen-year-old sister she told me she had recently had a cosmetic procedure performed. We were going through her first-year psychological science assignment together. Ironic. Kate wanted me to read through the criteria with her to ensure she understood what she was being asked to do. We were talking through the referencing guidelines, and I was adding comments left, right and centre. There was a pause in conversation. I didn't notice because I was too entranced by the art of Microsoft Word and connecting with my sibling beyond her stealing my favourite shirt and telling me I had a bigger nose than her.

'Hannah.'

'Kate.'

'I've been avoiding telling you something because I know you'll be really angry with me.'

'Let's get it over with then,' I said, deadpan. I was deleting a rogue capital letter and not giving her the time of day as I moved to the next proof point.

'I got chin filler a couple of months ago and I know it is expensive and stupid and you are going to hate me for it but you have insecurities too and you complain about them but I just decided to change mine so what's the big deal surely that's still feminist isn't it?' She finally came up for air. I thought she was going to hang up on me as a coping mechanism after that freestyle rap attempt.

I looked at the girl I helped toilet train when I was nine. My facial expression has never hidden anything, ever. I felt like a fucking failure.

My baby sister, the girl who had turned eighteen two months earlier, had paid more than $400 to cosmetically alter her appearance with injections. Kate had just come to me asking for money to fix the brake pads on her car but had prioritised spending her own earnings on creating a jawline she didn't believe she had. In a cost-of-living crisis, she still put her appearance before her livelihood. I was not angry about the money; I was distraught that she felt she needed to prioritise that.

'It'll only last six months, so don't worry,' Kate reassured me.

Right, I thought. So you have done something that does not have lasting effects so you'll go back to pay for it time and time again in the pursuit of a thin and youthful look you are currently experiencing in peak form. I started googling the procedure as she was speaking, to understand what had actually been inserted into her skin and how different clinics described the procedure. The first Sydney clinic's site read, 'Dermal fillers are used to add volume and prominence to small and weak chins'; the website directly underneath explained that, 'Some people were born with a great profile including a well projected chin, and others were born with underdeveloped or recessive chins whose appearance could be improved. For those who were not born with the perfect chin, it is simple to just inject them with chin fillers to improve the appearance.'

But I couldn't get into that. Instead, I asked: 'Okay, and how do you feel?'

'Better. Can you not tell the difference – see?' She angled the camera to a profile view, showing me the same face I had looked at with love for eighteen years. There was no visible difference.

'Not at all, Kate. You have a beautiful face. I never would have noticed the change.'

'Well, I can tell, and anyway the lady said we could try more millilitres next time because there's more work to be done.'

Of course she said that. She's not going to tell an eighteen-year-old forking out to feel pretty and worthy via having chemicals injected into her head that she's beautiful just the way she is. There's no world where she'd say, 'That's all done! You can now live happily ever after without ever facing another insecurity after this one mil of liquid has altered the course of your life as you know it.' But again, I bit my tongue.

'So you're happy?' I asked.

'Yes.'

'I'm glad.'

'Are you?' Her nerves made her voice crack.

'No, but that's not helpful right now. I'm sad you felt you

needed to do that – I feel like I've let you down by how much we talk about how we look.'

'Hannah, you have not let me down. I've let *you* down.'

But it was not on us; of course it wasn't.

The pursuit of beauty had implicitly damaged the tether between us. My sister had withdrawn so obviously from our relationship in the weeks before telling me, so terrified of what I might say or think about her. Beauty is something women are convinced we can buy, thereby improving our lives, building our confidence. Instead the purchase had bred shame in my sister, and divided us. The obvious conclusion might be that the shame was derived from my judgement, not the act itself, but our breakdown was not about my prospective judgement: it was in her feelings regarding her own decision. My younger sister had made a choice to override an insecurity, but I think the decision to do so became a new one.

I do not want any individual woman to feel shame for changing their appearance; instead I want us to challenge our silence around the decision to do so. What if instead of harbouring shame around these pressures and decisions, we ensure that criticism is only of the industry that cultivates our self-hatred? Our shame is their profit. The inability to speak to each other transparently about these feelings and experiences only allows them to fester. Women wanting to be beautiful and then feeling guilty for striving for it is another symptom of the problem. Disconnection from other women is disconnection from ourselves; it only works to lead us further down the patriarchal path.

One day, when I was thirteen and in the car being driven to school, my dad looked over at me from the driver's side. He sighed. 'You know, if we had the money, I would pay to get that nose fixed.'

My nose was the part of myself I had wanted to change most, and this desire was being validated by the person who made me. Only in recent months have I actually been able to look at an image of myself with a view of my profile and feel comfortable. My nose and my height had always been things that made me feel as though I literally 'stuck out' in every way.

I have always been very tall, and the language used to describe women's bodies always meant that the way I was described by family and friends felt like this was the worst thing I could be. Big, huge, enormous and large were all thrown around every time I walked into a function, birthday or gathering. The language defined me. I have men's size 13 feet (because a women's 15 does not exist), and I wore drag queen heels to my school formal. I looked at every image of myself and thought, *I look like I'm about to eat my friends.* I had no perception of how to intuitively eat because I needed more fuel than the girls at school, but not as much as the boys. As soon as I began starving myself, my hunger cues became incredibly difficult to navigate. Still now, I feel the effects of a decade of disordered eating – I struggle to work out when I'm hungry and when to stop. I grew up in a household where you finished the food on your plate. I often wonder how this demand to leave nothing behind affected the way I approach food. I used to eat as fast as possible to get it all down, as if it were my last meal. Now, I don't know how or what to eat, or even how to gauge if my disordered tendencies are flaring up again.

My relationship with my body has always reflected my relationship with control. Naomi Wolf said, 'A culture fixated on female thinness is not an obsession about female beauty, but an obsession about female obedience. Dieting is the most potent political sedative in women's history; a quietly mad population is a tractable one.' I must control which photos are posted and deleted. I must count and control calories. I must control the hair that grows on my body. I must choose clothes and outfits, not considering what makes me feel comfortable or good, but considering whether a garment is 'flattering'. My curls. The concealment of acne. The expectation of makeup. When our brains are occupied with hating ourselves, we have less intellectual capacity to challenge the system that monetises that feeling. I was not happier when I was in a smaller body; I just picked apart more, different things. The things I hated most about myself are the things I have come to find have defined how I am recognised now.

In the months leading up to the release of my first book, *Bite Back*, I experienced severe acne for the first time in my life. This was combined with significant hair loss and weight gain. While I worked hard to combat the thoughts that swirled around my bathroom scales, my lumpy face sucked me into a vortex of insecurity. I had always had pimples and a terrible relationship with skincare, but this eczema that began around my eyes bred into a full-scale takeover of my face. At the same time, I was posting videos on constitutional law in the lead-up to the referendum. Following one particular post, I had more than eighty people message me unsolicited advice on 'fixing' or 'helping' the face I was fronting the camera with to try to educate them for free. They diagnosed me with cystic acne. They told me it looked sore and they 'just wanted to help'. I had not asked – in fact, it was an active effort to continue showing up as I was – but they made sure I knew that I looked bad.

While visiting a dermatologist after being referred for a melanoma check on my back, she turned to me and stated matter-of-factly: 'Your back is fine, but we have to deal with your face. You cannot walk around in public looking like that.'

I wish people felt more shame for commenting on others' bodies, women especially. It cuts deep. While her communication might have meant: 'As a professional, I want to help you feel confident in your appearance,' her language communicated: 'It is shameful to look like that – hide yourself.' When men objectify, sexualise and offend, it rolls off me quicker. I do not want to fuck you and I do not want you to look at me. I could not care less about the opinion of the footy guy who uses a foot cream on his face. He will make someone very unhappy one day, and I feel more for her than myself. When a man tells me he does not want to have sex with me, in my mind at least, that means I am less likely to be sexually assaulted by him: win.

When women comment, it hits a nerve far deeper. They have lived experience. We share these feelings and insecurities and we know the pain it causes. It feels more personal, because what do they get from it? Who are they helping us pose for? Often, these women offer 'advice' in pursuit of money they are trying to coax out of us. (Ever been to a laser clinic where they loudly suggest at reception that you add on the anal package? Horrifying.) Or because they want to enforce shame. I am reminded that we have been trained by a system of patriarchy to take up as little space as possible and to do so beautifully. As a woman capable of sharing her opinions with only minimal regard for how I appear while doing this, it fascinates me how women want to improve my image. My lack of makeup and styling has distracted them from the point. In order to be heard clearly, please be more beautiful. In order to make your point, hide your blemishes from my gaze. 'I'm just trying to help you.' No, you are not. By commenting on my appearance, you shackle me to the system you abide by. I am trying to escape it, and I'm failing. I am trying to help you escape it: we are both failing.

But I'm not stating anything new. We know that social media is poisoning our self-image. Ground-breaking, profound thought. We know that generation Z, while more likely to see a mental-health practitioner and more progressive than generations before, are still falling victim to the entrapments of impossible beauty standards. Our screen time is directly correlated with the increase in eating disorders, cosmetic procedures and even an unhealthy obsession with skincare practices. In 2024, I argue that the transition from dieting and weight-loss culture in our feeds to excessive, overpriced skincare marks a faux-progressive distancing from a problematic culture of body dysmorphia to a campaign that extends and refreshes an age-old shaming of women: anti-ageing.

I am anti-botox and against getting any cosmetic procedures, which feels like an incredibly controversial statement to make in 2024. Let me make this clear: being 'anti-botox' does not make me critical of those who elect to have cosmetic procedures. I do not believe women should do anything to alter their appearance to be respected, employable, successful or considered 'beautiful'. I want those who elect to get these procedures for aesthetic reasons to be transparent about it. In a world where 'baby botox' is rife and labiaplasty is one of the fastest-growing cosmetic procedures in the world, I believe it is our responsibility to ourselves and the next generation to interrogate the industries that want us to be skinny, small and frozen in time. They want to exhaust us physically, mentally, emotionally and financially. This is not about choice or individual agency: it's about capitalism and patriarchy.

A 2023 study by the University of South Australia found that of the 238 young Australian women aged eighteen to twenty-nine surveyed, 16 per cent had already received cosmetic surgery and 54 per cent were considering having it in the future. My sister is not in a minority; she's a product of our generation. The data reveals a sharp increase in cosmetic procedures to alter appearances: between 2010 and 2018 procedures doubled from 117,000 to 225,000. When the report was released, seven million Australian adults were considering altering their appearance through cosmetic procedures in the next decade.

It is no great mystery why. TikTok's 'ageing filter', which was described by dermatologists as one of the most accurate depictions of the skin and facial features of our older selves, has been used 27.7 million times and counting. 'Sephora kids' is a widely known trend, with ten-year-olds now flooding beauty and skincare stores to buy expensive anti-ageing products that will damage their skin. According to the data platform Statista, between now and 2028, revenue from the baby and child skin-care market is expected to grow at a rate of nearly 6 per cent each year. As Phillippa Diedrichs, professor of psychology at the University of the West of England, told *The Guardian*, part of the issue is the expansion of how accessible these procedures are and who offers them: 'botox is now advertised at the dentist.' In Liz Plank's Substack piece, 'Can a feminist get botox?', she discusses a lesser-known reality of this cosmetic alteration.

The most worrying and least discussed danger (in my opinion) is that botox does not just change our faces, it transforms how we feel emotions. New research has found that injections can limit our ability to express certain feelings because our facial muscles simply aren't able to execute them. Because a core part of human communication is mirroring each other's emotional expressions, botox can mean we have trouble empathizing with one another. When certain parts of our faces are frozen, it can quite literally make us appear more cold.

The obvious counter-argument to this is, 'But you wear makeup, so what's the difference?'

Makeup is also an alteration. If we really drill down into it, so is wearing sunscreen and painting our toenails. Eating and changing clothes also change our physical appearance every single day. There is a clear spectrum of alteration and decision-making. I see a distinction between tinted sunscreen and having a needle penetrate your skin to fill you with toxins to paralyse your facial features in the pursuit of a perpetually youthful appearance. I do agree that makeup has deep repercussions for gender equality – but it is also an art form that has been largely reclaimed. Makeup is now definitively understood to be a centrepiece of performance art, entertainment, drag and theatre. We are also slowly seeing a transition into acceptance of boys and men wearing makeup, and women choosing not to. While I do not believe any person should feel the need to wear makeup in their day-to-day life in order to feel professional or receive workplace privileges because of their appearance, using foundation and an eyebrow pencil for a work function is significantly different to injecting plastic in your chin to change the geography of your face.

I do not believe makeup is entirely exempt from challenge, having experienced at nineteen a boss who sent me home for looking 'sick' when I just wasn't wearing mascara that day. But the health risks, complications, costs, level of alteration and permanency of cosmetic procedures is vastly different to wearing makeup.

No one should be treated differently for any choice not to engage with the beauty industry, but the high risks associated with procedures like breast implants and augmentation, and the reported side effects (fatigue, difficulty breathing, slurred speech and muscle paralysis) associated with botox illustrate the seriousness of these decisions we make. There is a line between superficial application and surgical alteration. While all these behaviours play, in some way, to the gaze of patriarchy, the costs, the risks and the pain associated with makeup versus cosmetic procedures sit on opposite ends of the scale.

When women do not have botox, they are called old. When women have enough botox that it is noticeable, that is considered a different category of ugly or undesirable by all members of society. I'm interested in the relationship between the projection of ourselves and our actual selves. I refuse to criticise an individual for their personal decision to alter their physical appearance. But I disagree with the stance that because it is a choice, botox is a feminist act. We know choice feminism, which supports the view that anything a woman does is inherently feminist, is a 'get out of jail free card' that removes our responsibility and subsequently undermines our agency in distinguishing right from wrong. It is impossible to detach these choices from the broader social context we exist in that tells all people, and predominantly women, that their bodies are something to be fixed. By getting botox, we are contributing to patriarchy, and I believe it's in a more significant way than by using makeup or skincare.

Men want women to have enough work done to not look their age, but not so much that it's clear they've altered themselves. Ah, the dichotomy of a 'natural' beauty. It's wealth and privilege concealed. Whether it's Ozempic or Brazilian butt lifts (you'll see them called BBLs), my primary concern is not that the act is antifeminist, but that it allows a cohort of the world's rich and famous to create and uphold a standard of beauty that others will damage their health trying to achieve. In the process, teenage girls will go into debt for a body they can't achieve – a body they will risk their lives to achieve. I often wonder if people are obsessed with meeting social beauty standards and if they actually feel better in smaller, altered bodies – or if they are just obsessed with the privileges that come with them.

This is an individual choice, and I am not asking you to stop. Many of my friends have had work done. But I want you to think about what your choice means. What does it mean for your finances? What does it mean for your mental health? Why is our first instinct to change ourselves physically, rather than attempt to change our psychology towards ourselves?

Of the first fifteen TikToks I watched this morning in bed, eight were related to skincare and beauty, four were related to running and the other three focussed on Taylor Swift. Meanwhile, my Instagram reels think I'm a Christian woman interested in celibacy and repenting for my sins. This is confusing, considering that algorithms are supposed to be collecting data about us at every moment, and using that data to serve us material that confirms our biases. While the content on my feed is often contradictory to my views, I don't believe that tradwives are being fed feminist dialogue in their feeds. In her book *Doppelganger*, Naomi Klein describes the importance of 'unselfing' within a cultural paradigm developing more narcissistic and egomaniac tendencies than ever before: 'We're being fed ourself back to us … the algorithm is a house of mirrors, just giving you more of what you did last time, it is all these loops. Keep being the version of you over and over and over again at infinitum.' I logically know I am fed the content I engage with, but sometimes, I wonder if the algorithms aspire to killing this part of me, to ensuring I hate myself more than I already do. To delivering me less of what actually propels me forwards, and instead ensuring that I am stuck at a standstill, too fixated on how I look to remember that what matters is what I'm saying.

This is the language of our social feeds. Anti-ageing. Ozempic.

High cortisol. Divine femininity. Tradwife. Clean girl aesthetic. Girl math. Fitspo. Bold Glamour filter. Pick me. Botox crying face. All of these terms are steeped in racial and gender inequality that belittles the experiences of women and gender diverse people. Thirteen-year-olds are being served 'antiwrinkle straws' by the algorithm of an app they view on their phone. Eleven-year-olds are taught that periods are something to be hidden from boys, who should never see them carrying the health products that help manage their comfort. Meanwhile, 2024 research from Dublin City University's antibullying centre shows that it only takes twenty-three minutes before sixteen- to eighteen-year-old boys on TikTok and YouTube Shorts are fed misogynistic content. The data showed that masculinist, antifeminist and extremist content was being delivered to accounts that were not looking to access this content, within minutes. Girls are being taught to hide their bodies, while boys are being taught to sexualise them – and far worse.

Meanwhile, a breast cancer awareness campaign was labelled pornography. A branded Bodyform campaign for period products was muted by social media for 'sexual content' in 2023, so the company launched a response detailing the forty words of women's health that are censored within our algorithms including 'clitoris', 'vulva', 'discharge', 'menopause', 'miscarriage' and 'polycystic ovary syndrome'. This is medical language; this is health literacy. When our bodies are deemed offensive, pornographic and explicit, what feelings do we internalise about them?

Taboo

When our body image is at its lowest, when we are overworked and undervalued, after we have been targeted with ad after ad, product after product, the wellness industry comes into focus. I am tired of scrolling past rich thin white model after rich thin white model on social media telling me that putting my phone down and not looking in the mirror is the key to joy. I resent the fact that women are told we need to reclaim time for ourselves and block out our body image issues by the same people who, consciously or not, perpetuate them. We are then told the final frontier to achieving inner peace is a $5000 wellness retreat, a bath bomb and another beauty supplement.

While many aspects of the wellness industry actually involve science-based health practices, the vast majority is surface-level 'self-care', which props up an industry to the tune of US$4.5 trillion globally, according to the Global Wellness Institute. The reason it works is because beauty, wellness and self-help profiteers have convinced women that this is our community, our safe space in society. I believe women of all ages who exist in social media spaces can fall victim to this, but it feels like a primarily generation Z and millennial experience. We are being told that peace can be achieved through breathwork and mindfulness, without considering how a forty-hour work week, thirty-six hours of unpaid labour, the mental load and a dying planet affect our psyches.

In her piece 'We're sedating women with self-care: how we became obsessed with wellness' for *The Guardian*, Katherine

Rowland explores the work of Rina Raphael, journalist and author of *The Gospel of Wellness*. Raphael argues that the industry of wellness has developed a cult following through certainty. 'They say, "I can definitely help you. This supplement is definitely going to cure your symptoms. You should try this diet. It'll get rid of all your pain." This is what gets people and hooks them in.' Rowland explores the work beyond just the mass appeal of the 'cure':

Raphael takes her reasoning a step further and argues that wellness has become a new form of faith. As organized religion has retreated from everyday life, she argues, wellness has rushed in to fill the void. 'It's providing belonging, identity, meaning, community. These are all the things that people used to find in their neighbourhood church or synagogue. Wellness offers some sort of salvation on the horizon.' It also offers the illusion of control and empowerment. 'If you work hard enough and you buy the right things, you'll be saved from disease and ageing and anything bad happening to you,' Raphael says … To believe that you are at the helm can offer respite from the constant deluge of technology, screaming children and a burning planet. But an illusion it remains. Even the best laid plan of diet, exercise and sobriety will dictate only a small portion of health outcomes, because it simply pales in comparison to systemic factors, including the spillage of work into all waking hours, the orange haze that consumes the skies, and the lopsided hazards and opportunities that hew to how much you earn, or the color of your skin.

We have become slaves to our own self-improvement. The language of the self-help industry imposes a belief that the reason you do not feel 'well' is because you are not investing enough time, money and energy into the capitalism of self-improvement when the reality is much more sinister. I would go as far as to say we are better-versed in the *language* of therapy than in actual self-improvement and growth practices. We now use language such as 'trauma', 'triggered', 'gaslight' and 'heal' after watching social media bites of therapy without actually engaging in therapy and therefore utilising the language we are wielding accurately.

We are constantly speaking about cultivating joy, boosting productivity and making space for self-love without actually addressing any of the actual underlying issues of living in a world that takes everything from us and asks us to connect with ourselves through an overpriced candle that smells like the inside of a barn. To call out this institution of marketing and smokescreens is one of the biggest taboos, because while most women understand the moral questions around the beauty industry, 'wellness' and 'self-care' are framed through the language of medicine and healing.

We are encouraged to blame ourselves for our unhappiness, our circumstances, our appearance and our perceived defects. Dismantling taboo is working to ensure that we blame the system, not women. It is not our responsibility to completely detach from an ecosystem of expectations we have always existed in, but it is our duty to ourselves and everyone around us to question and critique the constant harmful messaging we are presented. It is your responsibility to your body, your mind and the people you influence to consider how you talk about your appearance. Beauty regimens, dieting and other cosmetic alterations are a personal choice, but when driven by self-hatred, how informed are we to actually choose? How can we truly have the agency to decide, when we are engulfed in a world that wants us to hate ourselves?

I have so desperately wanted to give in, to change and change and change, to pay my way to a false sense of satisfaction. But who wins? I believe it is a bandaid solution that only momentarily conceals the realities of ageing, of a growing and changing body, and of my own issues. I am not going to feel more beautiful in departing from who I am physically. I'll spend a lifetime disappointed that I can never escape the thoughts I'm feeding myself on TikTok each and every day. Instead, I'd rather find out what sits beneath all that. I want to disengage from messaging that tells me I'll be more worthy of love, more likely to be in a relationship or to find success, if I just get my eyebrows tattooed on, my buccal fat removed or take a weight-loss drug that will destroy my relationship with food. I'm going to question that messaging. I know the key to combating these thoughts is not a physical change, but a mental one.

taboo 2:

✗

The Health Gap

At the beginning of last year, I was approached by a brand whose owners wanted me to partner with them to promote period products. They wanted me to help them sell more pads and tampons; I wanted to earn money by helping to sell good pads and tampons. Easy, I thought. I'll be able to educate people on the menstrual cycle, make some funny jokes and continue doing my job talking frankly about politics, law, sex, relationships and power. This is my cup of tea.

Then the creative brief came in.

Can you deliver an advertisement that aligns with our campaign? It's all about empowerment. Ways that you feel liberated when menstruating. The slide deck they sent was covered in the words *WOMEN, FEMINIST* and *EMPOWERED.* It had imagery of feminist fillms and power suits from slide to slide of the powerpoint.

I know the brand meant well and that marketing through empowerment can be incredibly impactful. But I do not want to sell to someone that bleeding in itself is empowering or liberating or feminist. It just is. It is neutral. Period products went from being taboo, shameful and largely invisible to suddenly being a part of the capitalist girlboss agenda. Are we ever just allowed to exist without it being shameful or marketable? Can we simply just be?

I shut my laptop, picked a serious wedgie and went home. I decided to cook myself the thickest chicken schnitzel in the packet and a family serving of packet alfredo. I stirred the cream in, seething. I need to earn money to continue doing what I'm doing – but at what fucking cost to the kind of feminist conversations I am aiming to have? I thought I was a sell-out for considering it.

I knew, as I pulled my favourite plate-bowl out of the cupboard, that this partnership would come at the cost of fifteen-year-old me, who put a tampon in for the first time on a school trip, angled the object completely wrong and walked around in debilitating pain for hours. I didn't even have my period; I thought I just might and so shoved it in and pulled it out dry. I didn't feel comfortable asking anyone how to use a tampon. I haven't used one since. I didn't feel *empowered to menstruate* as I hobbled around with a bullet-shaped puff ball of pain sideways in my privates.

It would also come at the cost of nineteen-year-old me, who tried to feel confident enough to be touched by a boy who found my period disgusting. I didn't feel particularly liberated as he looked at the blood on his finger and tried to hide a clear expression of revulsion. I didn't even realise I had started my cycle.

It would come at the cost of twenty-five-year-old me, who has been getting a period for seven days every fourteen days due to a contraceptive implant that is not working with my body. I don't feel like a girlboss getting my iron infusion so I can stand up without getting dizzy every day. I wasn't particularly strengthened by spending in excess of $500 to have hormones released into my body that gave me the payoff of no baby in exchange for crying and bleeding every second week for months on end.

I take issue with the fact that these types of period problems are considered normal – they shouldn't be our standard experiences of our menstrual cycles. But I don't want to run a campaign on the girlbossery of shedding the lining of my internal organs. I can't argue with a straight face that I am enhanced when bleeding down my leg while at a work event or ruining my linen sheet set because I wanted to have sex with my partner on a Saturday morning. I just want to get my period and make it through the day feeling fine. I just want a product that works.

It isn't just young people who aren't equipped with the

education to understand our bodies, limiting our ability to use the language required to advocate for them. A *New York Times* piece on menstrual knowledge by Alisha Haridasani Gupta reported that a 2020 survey of American paediatricians, who are required to educate preteens about their menstrual cycles, found that a third did not know the median age menstruation begins, with a fifth not being able to identify whether there was a minimum age that menstruators could begin wearing tampons. On the article's test of ten questions, I scored 4.5. I am a woman who has had a period for a decade and used three forms of contraceptive, and I still know very little about the function of my reproductive organs. We have more pink Instagram tiles 'raising awareness' than ever, but not the knowledge or education to shed the vulnerability we feel around normal bodily functions.

One month into a new relationship, I asked my partner if he would download my period tracking application. I use the app daily to input my mood, my discharge consistency, how my digestion is flowing, whether I've had sex or masturbated and even my exercise patterns and alcohol consumption. This is my way of assessing whether particular symptoms and emotional experiences I'm having are aligned with my menstruation. The app, I had just discovered, has a feature that allows partners to pair their phone to a person's account, and receive notifications as to where their partner is at in their cycle, including common symptoms and hormonal experiences. Basically, bring home the groceries today, do not make insensitive comments tomorrow, when you tapped my bum last week in the kitchen I wanted to have sex with you there and then but if you do it on Sunday I'll need to lie down and count to ten to not cry. Brace for emotional impact sort of stuff. I felt nervous to ask, not because I actually thought there would be an issue, but because it felt like emotional labour for him. Ridiculous, isn't it? That something built to help him understand me better by having an awareness of my bodily functions would make me feel guilty? This should be entirely normalised – not celebrated but expected.

He immediately downloaded the app and requested the code that would link him to the limited information from the symptoms I inputted. When I copied the code to text him, the app provided me with a template text to share with the link.

Join me on Flo for Partners to supercharge our sex life and connect better.

Immediately, I was alarmed. I felt hot, burning rage in my tummy. It could have been the spicy Guzman chicken burrito from four hours before, but I remain quite sure it was fury. This application decided, from data or from belief, that the best way to incentivise men to give a flying fuck about their partners' menstruation and hormonal experiences was to advertise knowledge sharing as a way to improve sexual experiences. Menstruating bodies are not something for men to 'hack'. They may claim it will assist in planning for pregnancy or the feeling of being turned on – but the salient message of that communication is: do this to get more. Is this how men need to be convinced to learn about their partners' bodies? Am I being hypersensitive for caring about the way we promote improved knowledge and care factor? These questions are important – what role does pragmatism play in social change? Seeing as the Cancer Council advertises sunscreen with anti-ageing messaging, is it acceptable to work for an uptake in men caring about menstruation by bribing them with the hope of extra sex?

Men are never taught about women's fertility and reproductive organs, and I'd go as far as to say that those who understand this basic biology are perceived by patriarchy as being weaker 'simps', which is internet slang for a man who is submissive, affectionate and attentive towards a romantic partner or love interest. Men are mocked by other men for caring about women at all, let alone about our reproductive organs and how our cycles impact us, but the world also ignores the role men's health plays in fertility. Men's sexual organs are socially acceptable, but discussing male-specific infertility is not. Most of the world wouldn't know this, but sperm counts have halved in the last fifty years – and the decline is accelerating. This is a public health crisis whose cause scientists are still working on establishing, with the early belief that pollution, alcohol, diet and stress are just some of the primary contributors. One of the best reads on the topic is 'How pollution is causing a male fertility crisis' by Katherine Latham for the BBC. Getting straight to the data:

> Sperm count, explains Levine, is closely linked to fertility chances. While a higher sperm count does not necessarily mean a higher probability of conception, below the 40 million/ml threshold the probability of conception drops off rapidly. In 2022, Levine and his collaborators published a review of global trends in sperm count. It showed that sperm counts fell on average by 1.2% per year between 1973 to 2018, from 104 to 49 million/ml. From the year 2000, this rate of decline accelerated to more than 2.6% per year.

If that was too many numbers (it was for me, I read it three times), basically: sperm count has declined by 51.6 per cent in five decades, and, if the decline continues, we are facing a significant decrease in the global capacity for reproduction. This is a worldwide phenomenon, and yet no one seems to be talking about it. When I think about my own fertility, I realise I know very little of the science. What I know is fear. I know I am supposed to be afraid of ageing, of infertility, of regretting not having children if I so choose (or the shame and grief so many women experience when they want to have children but cannot). Fear of the guilt of returning to work, and the fear of losing myself and my financial independence if I do not.

I know that every comments section around any post on parenting is the scariest place I've ever been and it isn't relevant to me at all. (Have you ever read a community group post from your hometown about when babies should start eating solids? Fucking hell.) I am an educated, privileged mid-twenties woman, but what I actually understand of fertility is only the mental load and shame that women are taught to carry. We bear the responsibility of family making and managing.

Earlier this year, federal treasurer Dr Jim Chalmers stated that it would be 'better' if birth rates were higher in our country, in the lead-up to announcing a 2024 budget he said would be 'for mothers'. Our national focus is on reproduction, but not enough to close our health gaps, to improve reproductive access, to make healthcare and fertility treatments affordable or to alleviate the costs associated with actually raising children in a cost-of-living crisis. While this labour and its distribution will be explored later, the reproductive taboos and factors surrounding our choice to become parents still remains largely undiscussed. It is a territory many are terrified to chart. I can't think of a time in my childhood when I comprehended parenthood from any other angle.

Last year, my brain chemistry was altered at the Sydney Opera House's All About Women festival. I attended an exceptional panel called Maybe Baby, featuring Gina Rushton, Dr Natasha Andreadis and Brooke Boney, which was moderated by Sana Qadar. The panellists spoke about reproductive choice, climate anxiety, fertility science and relationship breakdowns when it comes to discussions around parenthood. It was pragmatic and real and dismantled complex taboos in a way I had never encountered. I learned that recent research suggests only 7–10 per cent of women who freeze their eggs come back for them, the others paying tens of thousands of dollars for a service they do not ever utilise. Is this because we are so frightened by the misinformation we see online that we take unnecessary action?

According to a report from late 2023, four in five Australians want more fertility education. We are constantly 'raising awareness' without sufficient education of a range of women's, transgender and non-binary people's health experiences and conditions. Men's health, more broadly, exists at the centre of our world. Historically, men have been the only subjects of many medical studies, yet the place they are most invisible are the subjects in which there is any opportunity to place responsibility on women, especially contraception and fertility. The complete silence around 'spermaggedon' is a symptom of a larger problem: that the burden of family planning is placed wholly on women in heterosexual relationships. This does not begin when the pregnancy is contemplated or even when the child is born, but when we as little girls begin to internalise the belief that motherhood is the headline of our life.

Not only does this confine women to a place in our community where I do not believe we are valued, centred or included, it also denies men the opportunity to feel comfortable to discuss their fears, their desires, their emotions and the opportunity to challenge the system that sees them as the secondary carer or, worse, accommodates their absence. We do not just have an orgasm gap, but a reproductive gap. Women have limited knowledge of our own cycles, fertility and long-term experiences of our reproductive symptoms. But men know far less – and this starts with early education. I confidently said Genovia was a real country in a grade eight geography test, and boys in my year twelve class confidently told me that you only need to use a condom during a period because that's when the pregnancy risk is.

Women work hard to remain the objects of men's desire, and men can barely be convinced to learn where the clitoris is. But we all need to better understand women's health, because our sex lives, our reproductive rights and our relationships depend on it. While these subjects are considered taboo, they affect men greatly. In a PsychWire interview for her book, *How The Pill Changes Everything: Your Brain on Birth Control*, Dr Sarah E. Hill outlines the way the contraceptive pill can alter women's perceptions and attraction to men:

> When women are on the pill, this can affect men in two ways. First, because the pill suppresses ovulation, it also suppresses many of the fertility-related cues that men find desirable in women. For example, research

indicates that men find women sexier and more de[sirable]
near ovulation compared to other points in the cycle.
Research also finds that being around ovulating women
increases men's levels of testosterone. Accordingly, the
pill may decrease men's attraction to their partners by
suppressing women's mid-cycle spike in sexiness and
preventing cycle-based testosterone boosts. This could
change men's behavior in lots of different ways, ranging
from how they treat their partners to how they respond
to competitive challenges (testosterone increases
competitiveness).

A second way that it can impact men is through the
changes it has on women's sexual decision making. The
pill – because it prevents pregnancy almost without
fail – is linked with greater sexual unrestrictedness in
women. This means women are more willing to have
casual sex with men than they used to be, and that
their standards for what an acceptable sex partner has
to have achieved, have declined. This has been great
for women and women's liberation, in general, but it
may have the unintended effect of robbing men of the
single biggest motivator of male achievement known to
man: the fear of involuntary celibacy. Motivating men
to achieve obviously isn't women's JOB (and it is the
fault of men, not women, if men are not able to achieve
the way that they once were). However, the pill may

have played one small role in the growing achievement gap between men and women.

After decades of hard-won destigmatisation – transitioning 'sanitary products' to 'period products' in grocery stores; normalising the sale of vibrators in chemists and clothing stores – corporate machines step in and open their cash registers. When a taboo around sex and reproduction is broken down over time, brands are able to commodify this by making billions telling women their bodies are a well of empowerment ready to be accessed. Period product companies argue that our menstrual cycle has been normalised because ten minutes ago they started using red water instead of blue to test them in advertisements. But I do not think slapping *LIBERATION*, *CHOICE* and *EMPOWERMENT* on everything from tampons to eye cream is evidence of a significant shift. We move from being dirty to divine through pink-washing practices to earn the men at the top of these corporations millions. Shame or capitalise: choose.

When we discuss this in relation to period care, we only scratch the surface of a raft of health issues and gaps that remain both taboo and commonplace: a lethal combination. The 'husband stitch' is just one example of violence against women that's sanitised through patriarchal language. This procedure still occurs around the world today, and involves doctors putting in an extra stitch 'for daddy' or 'for the husband' when repairing episiotomies or tearing following birth. It is medical malpractice and medical misogyny. This extra stitch is performed allegedly to tighten the vagina to increase sexual pleasure for a male partner. It can leave women in debilitating pain.

When we look at female genital mutilation more broadly, we see just how prevalent and silent a topic it remains. According to UNICEF:

> Female genital mutilation (FGM) refers to 'all procedures involving partial or total removal of the female external genitalia or other injury to the female genital organs for non-medical reasons.' FGM is a violation of girls' and women's human rights. Around the world, over 230 million girls and women have been cut. Africa accounts for the largest share of this total, with over 144 million. Asia follows with over 80 million, and a further 6 million are in the Middle East. Another 1-2 million are affected in small practising communities and destination countries for migration in the rest of the world.

On a weekly basis my TikTok feed presents women's anecdotes of these experiences. Women who have to ask for additional doctor's notes to give their husbands who pressure them into sex after traumatic births; women who discover why they've been experiencing painful sex during a pap smear when their practitioner tells them what their doctor did without consent; women whose doctors convinced them to get plastic surgery they didn't require without making them aware of the long-term effects of implants and procedures. We live in a society where we have not been medically emancipated from patriarchy.

The women's health gap doesn't just relate to our own understanding of our bodies, but the way we are medically diagnosed, treated and believed when we present with symptoms. Women presenting with symptoms of reproductive concern are routinely told to lose weight or offered antidepressants. In Australia, two-thirds of women report bias or discrimination in Australian healthcare, according to the End Gender Bias survey, which engaged more than 2500 participants. The findings show that demeaning interactions occurred specifically during intimate examinations and childbirth, instances involving higher levels of vulnerability. Notably, four in five LGBTQIA+ survey respondents and over 80 per cent of women with a disability reported discrimination and bias, compared to around 67 per cent of other women.

The World Economic Forum provides key research on how and why we continue to fail women. One of the primary examples is the gender health gap in heart attacks:

Women in the UK are around a third less likely to receive a coronary angiogram (which allows doctors to see narrowing or blockages in blood vessels) after a STEMI heart attack, mainly caused by heart disease. A study published in *The Lancet Regional Health – Europe* found that women were more likely to die after being admitted to hospital with a severe heart attack, but they were also less likely to be prescribed medication to prevent future heart attacks, such as statins. Previous research has found women were 50% more likely than men to be given an incorrect diagnosis following a heart attack.

The research outlines five conditions that emphasise the gravity of these global medical failures. Three times as many boys than girls are diagnosed with autism, because of different presentations of the condition. According to the American Autoimmune Association, women account for 80 per cent of people with autoimmune diseases, but it takes, on average, five years for women to receive a diagnosis. This is all before we even begin to consider the underdiagnosed, under-researched and largely unknown realities of conditions such as endometriosis. According to McKinsey, merely 1 per cent of healthcare research in 2020 was invested in female-specific conditions beyond oncology.

Women's health is chronically underfunded and our pain is dismissed. Ending medical misogyny in Australia requires a multipronged approach to closing our health gaps – not only for women generally, but for disabled women, gender diverse people, First Nations women and beyond. In Melissa Davey's piece for *The Guardian* on tackling these systemic failures, she identifies unique issues our nation faces.

Aboriginal and Torres Strait Islander women are twice as likely to have cardiovascular disease and to die from coronary heart disease or stroke than non-Indigenous women. They also die 7.8 years earlier than non-Indigenous women ...

A survey of Australian cancer patients found 58% of trans and gender diverse respondents said fear of mistreatment was the biggest barrier when accessing healthcare and 20% said they had been refused general healthcare.

The article provides clear recommendations by health professionals on how to make tangible change in healthcare practices. One example is ending obstetric violence, which Western Sydney University research tells us impacted one in ten people who gave birth between 2017 and 2022. It also requires us to value and advance female participation in clinical trials, the lack of which has led to healthcare bias globally. Women are 75 per cent more likely to experience adverse reactions to prescription medications than men because of our distinct physical traits, according to Dr Laura Wilson.

When our pain and symptoms are so regularly dismissed, advocating for ourselves or even identifying that something might be wrong becomes exponentially more challenging. When reports of pain are not believed, we are taught not to value or identify that pain as indicating a need for medical attention or treatment. Long-term health outcomes can be significantly impacted by our unwillingness to seek the attention and care we require. Knowing that this is the reality of women's healthcare is vital to breaking the silence around our pain.

And how does this all bleed into our capacity for communication – and the extent to which we are heard – in other parts of our life? For me, it greatly impacted my experience and understanding of sex and my relationship with pleasure.

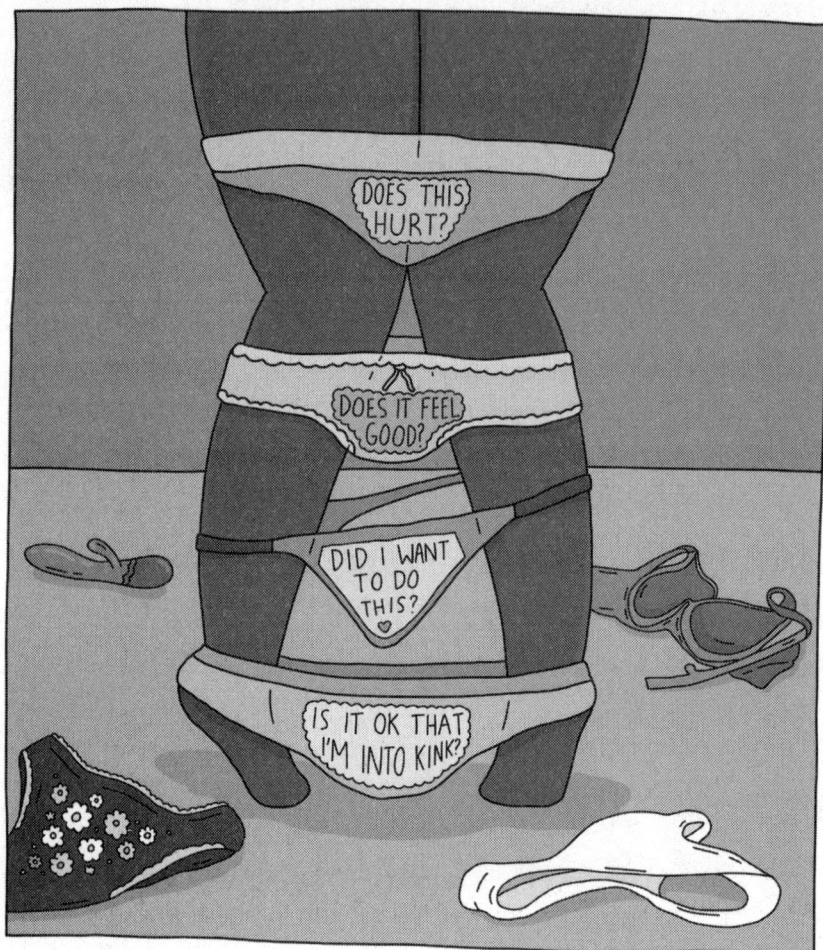

2
sex

taboo 3:

✖

Women's
Pleasure and Pain

'Stop having rough sex.'

That is what my female general practitioner advised. It was the first time I had ever talked to someone other than my previous long-term partner about the pain I was experiencing during sex.

I sat in the patient's chair, with my legs tightly crossed, in an attempt to stop my left foot from tapping. I looked firmly down at my knees as she typed. I had already stared at the healthy food pyramid poster and anatomical charts found in every one of these white-lit clinically soulless places. I had been working up the courage to tell a medical professional about what was going on for two years. It was why I had selected her on the practice website, because her bio described her as 'passionate about women's health and sexual health'. I clenched my hands into a tight ball as she printed me a prescription for the pill – the initial reason I had booked the appointment.

'I can only deal with one issue right now,' she said, handing me the paper. She smiled earnestly. 'But remember to use lubricant and have a glass of wine beforehand. It can help with the pain.'

I felt my cheeks begin to burn. My face was not flushed in a cute way – I was sweating through my work shirt. My jaw was completely clenched. The water in my eyes was being held back with the tightest restraint I could muster; I felt humiliated, and if I'd said one more word I knew the catch in my throat would trigger a burst of tears.

I was not having *any* sex, let alone rough sex.

I swiftly thanked her in a cheery and overly sanitised tone, grabbed my backpack, paid eighty-something dollars for the piece of paper that would just overload me with hormones as a response to me seeking help about excessive bleeding and contraceptive failure, and lined up at the pharmacy to get the prescription for the secondary hormonal contraceptive I needed – because I was not allowed to get my Implanon bar taken out after sixty days of straight bleeding, I needed to also go on the pill to try to 'recalibrate' my body. That's a topic for another book.

In the two years that followed that appointment, I had sex once.

The doctor was not the reason, but she had affirmed the story I had told myself to that point. Sex didn't feel good, which obviously meant there was something wrong with me. I didn't know how to communicate what I needed during sex, because I didn't know it was possible to have sober sex that felt good.

I had been scared of all forms of intimacy since I was a small child. I didn't want to be touched, to be kissed, to be cuddled. Closeness frightened me, because opening myself up meant that it could also be taken away. I didn't want to be seen naked by a sexual partner. I didn't want to ask anyone to help me use a tampon, so I never did. I still struggle to say 'I love you' to my mum and sister, even though they always gently say it to me at the end of every phone call – still trying, softly. My friends used to joke that they could only get a hug out of me on their birthdays.

When it came to having sex, I felt like a failure for never doing 'anything' until I was almost twenty-one. Now, I think that is a blessing. The pain I was experiencing; the level of alcohol I was consuming to engage in those experiences and to silence my debilitating inner critic; the lack of knowledge I had of how partnered sex can work: all that meant I was not emotionally equipped to talk myself through those experiences before, during or after. My entire concept of sober sex was fear, shame and crippling pelvic pain. My broader experience of sex was the belief that I was not going to enjoy it unless I was drunk. I was breaching my own consent. I was pushing through and past all my internal warning systems just so I'd have anecdotes to offer my friends, to look like I 'got it'. To not *feel* inexperienced or prudish or like the loser I felt I was for not having had a range of sexual partners and experiences. The reality of what I ultimately ended up with was low self-worth and a mistrust of men.

So when I now ask myself why I didn't push my doctor further, why I didn't advocate for myself, I can give myself grace. How could I have asked for something I didn't believe was possible for me?

I moved to Sydney the following year and found another female doctor who made me feel safe. I told her I had concerns around painful intercourse. She immediately referred me to a pelvic floor physiotherapist and a gynaecologist. Before attempting to perform a cervical screening test (the new name for a pap smear, which we happily chatted about for the whole appointment because I like going to the doctor as a way to better understand women's health), my GP gently asked me if I had experienced sexual trauma.

'Ah, not specifically one incident – but I suppose there have been bad times.'

Again, the siren internally alarming my body and brain said not to claim that space. Not to see my experiences as those of sexual violence. I blame myself for not saying no, despite knowing that for everyone else I stipulate that informed consent requires an ongoing, enthusiastic yes.

She was kind. This healthcare professional softly told me that, if I was comfortable, we could try to conduct the test and the STI screenings I also wanted to have completed that day.

'If it hurts, or at any point you want to stop, just let me know. The gynaecologist will be more equipped to help you navigate this.'

I almost started crying. To have an expert look me in the eyes with understanding was overwhelming. I lay down on the bed and she guided me slowly through the process. Within two minutes, she stopped.

'I can't find your cervix because you are tightening exactly as you said. It looks to me like vaginismus: you are right. I've got the swabs I need for your STI checks but I don't want to do anything unnecessary when you can see a women's health specialist first.'

Vaginismus. Finally.

Vaginismus is a condition where the vaginal muscles tighten or spasm involuntarily when something attempts to penetrate – like a tampon, a sex toy or a penis. Vaginismus is a psychosomatic condition, meaning it is caused or aggravated by mental factors. The pain I was experiencing was caused by my emotional distress, shame, embarrassment and fear of sex and my body. The only reason I knew about vaginismus was having listened to an episode of the Bumble podcast, *Love etc.*, in which Shameless Media Founder Zara McDonald spoke about her experience with the condition in the episode 'Actually, I hate sex'.

I didn't just *think* there was something wrong with my vagina: I believed it. I fundamentally believed that my body was wrong and that I was bad at sex. I had started having intercourse just before I turned twenty-one, and I felt ashamed of my lack of knowledge, experience and that – though I'd now found someone to try intimacy with – I was scared and in pain.

In all the sexual experiences I had leading up to a doctor actually listening to me and helping me, this was the story I told myself:

> I need to be drunk to enjoy sex. I need to push through the pain in order to give my partner the closeness we need. It is imperative that I have regular sex, because I am a young woman. This is something that I will get over if I just keep having sex. If I am not having sex, if I am not actively dating – I am not growing. I am not learning about myself.

My dad told me I was a lesbian who hated men at any point that I wasn't in a relationship. My mum said she was accepting she was not getting grandchildren. My friends knew I was hung up on someone I shouldn't have given a second date, let alone a year of my brain space. Only I knew I was terrified of letting someone touch me. I was twenty-four.

The next month, I took myself to a pelvic floor physiotherapist for an initial consult. In the space of forty-five minutes I went from never having inserted something inside myself without knife-blade-like pain to actively guiding my own stretching practices and purchasing dilators to aid my progress. The brilliant specialist I saw was incredibly patient and informed me through the best way that I could understand what was happening: language. We spoke through the associations I had made with sex; the words 'discomfort', 'pain' and 'fear' were the guiding infrastructure.

'The other thing is, since you've been on the contraceptive pill for so long, your bleeding is likely the result of poor skin quality at the opening of your vagina.'

'Wouldn't I know about that?'

'Well, you've been on the pill basically since you were fifteen. When you are on the pill for longer than a year, one key side effect is that the skin inside or at the opening of your vagina can become dry and susceptible to paper-cut-like tearing during sex.'

'That is what happens, because the blood does often seem to be just after I wipe, if that makes sense.'

'Exactly. So I can prescribe a cream called Ovestin, which can improve the skin quality and return it to a more plump, moist and healthy state.'

Oh my god. Why didn't I know this? Why had I been bleeding during sex for five years with no understanding beyond 'there's something wrong with me'?

Because female pleasure during sex is the lowest priority: it is a patriarchal taboo. Our safety, comfort and consent is barely a consideration for many men.

Research from the American College of Obstetricians and Gynaecologists revealed that 75 per cent of women have experienced painful sex at some point in their lifetime. This isn't just vaginismus but can be the result of a range of conditions ranging from birth trauma to a lack of foreplay. These are not inevitable features of sex, but are something people with vulvas often believe they must endure to 'perform' adequately during partnered intercourse with men.

In 2018, an article from the Australian Broadcasting Corporation proved the prevalence of painful sexual experiences for women, stating that a study of 20,000 people found one in five had endured painful intercourse for a period of at least one month in the twelve months preceding the survey.

I know that pain will specifically impact my sexual experience, for much of my life. From breastfeeding to childbirth, menopause, hormonal fluctuations, vaginal dryness, tearing and beyond, bodily changes will impact the sensations, comfort, pain and pleasure I experience during penetrative intercourse.

Comparatively, 2 per cent of men reported experiencing sexual pain in the same period. Men experience pain less than women, and more orgasms. The International Academy of Sex Research published data in 2017 stating 95 per cent of heterosexual men reported that they usually or always orgasmed when sexually intimate, followed by 89 per cent of gay men, 88 per cent of bisexual men, 86 per cent of lesbian women, 66 per cent of bisexual women and 65 per cent of straight women. In terms of sexual hierarchy, straight women quite literally come last. In discussing this data, Professor Laurie Mintz wrote for *The Conversation*:

> In one study of more than 50,000 people, 95% of heterosexual men said they usually or always orgasm when sexually intimate, while only 65% of heterosexual women said the same … In my work, I've asked thousands of women: 'What is your most reliable route to orgasm?' Only 4% say penetration. The other 96% say clitoral stimulation, alone or paired with penetration.

The female orgasm is not a mystery. The same piece reported that 92 per cent of women orgasm when pleasuring themselves. It also found that casual sex was less conducive to climax in women. Mintz wrote that in a study of more than 12,000 college students, one in ten of the women said they orgasm during first-time hookups while 68 per cent said they orgasm during sex that occurs in a committed relationship. The overwhelming majority of women are capable of reaching orgasm during solo sex.

I also do not believe orgasm is the goal of sex. That is a

view that lacks nuance and understanding of how pleasure and arousal occur, build and can be flattened. We are complex beings and a diagram of the clitoris isn't a magic-wand solution. What I do wonder, but don't know the conclusive answer to, is whether women are faking their way through partnered sexual experiences, or whether their partners are unresponsive to feedback.

It is our responsibility to give feedback and actively communicate our wants and our needs, and that requires us to have a positive sexual relationship with ourselves. Knowing what turns me on, what makes me feel safe and ensuring I never 'fake' pleasure with or hide pain from my partner allows our intimacy to thrive. If your partner does not care about your pleasure, run. But if you are distorting their understanding of your body by faking orgasms, how can you expect them to change their approach and meet your needs? Studies suggest between 50 and 85 per cent of women have faked an orgasm. I will be the first to say I have failed time and time again to advocate for myself and deliver on the suggestions I make. I am committed to making pleasure authentic, to never hiding pain or performing pleasure again in my life. I deserve that and my partner deserves that. That is authentic connection.

In a culture where women's pleasure has been made an afterthought, if not a source of shame, how are we supposed to train ourselves out of the conditioning that our needs come last? That experiencing pain or discomfort is not normal and not to be 'tolerated'? Women are more concerned with whether a vibrator will be delivered in discreet packaging than whether their sexual partner cares about their pleasure in the bedroom.

I'm not saying all men are like this, but all men benefit from it. In an interview for her global bestseller *Women Don't Owe You Pretty*, Florence Given said, 'Women are so focussed, not through our own choosing but through socialisation, on being polite that we have muted our intuition, to the point where we will be in a dangerous situation and feel guilty about assuming that this person is dodgy.'

This muted intuition doesn't just silence the internal alarms shrieking inside us, it also prevents us from leaning into pleasure entirely. I know how often my self-surveillance and fear have prevented me from being totally in my body, from releasing control and allowing sex to be an act that doesn't require a sucked-in stomach and the right tempo and diversity of moans. What if it was unrestricted joy? Sex is a mental act, and pleasure requires safety, understanding and connection. In order to sit entirely within our bodies and develop our relationship with solo and partnered pleasure it is vital that we know ourselves. Like all taboos, this starts with exploration and involves discomfort. Unrestricted joy requires vulnerability, because it demands letting our guard down.

understanding your pleasure

Ask yourself these questions and, if you feel comfortable, write down the answers.

1. Think of the best sex you've ever had. Try to create a vivid image in your mind. Describe the entire day it occurred on in detail. What happened surrounding the sex? Context is crucial. What parts of the sex made you feel best? How did your body feel? How did you emotionally feel? What was your favourite thing you did during this experience? If it was partnered sex, what did your partner do that made you feel pleasure?

2. Describe a moment where you felt turned on by something non-sexual. Was it a particular action or form of intimacy? Was it something you saw on the street or watched in a movie? Make a list of non-sexual objects and acts of intimacy that elicit a positive response in your body.

3. Explain the difference in how you feel during partnered sex from your feelings during solo pleasure. When you masturbate, articulate how the experience and feeling is distinct. Is it possible to bridge the gap between these feelings?

4. How do heteronormative society and gender norms affect your view of sex? Think of what you like during intercourse and how this may differ from what you have been taught is acceptable. Is there something you aren't exploring, or aren't asking for?

5. What is the difference between sex and love, in your opinion? What is your view on hookup culture?

6. What do you struggle to communicate during partnered sex, and why? What stops you asking for what you want? Do you seek feedback and do you provide it?

7. What does sex mean to you? Imagine explaining sex to someone who doesn't know what it is, who has never come across it. How would you help them to understand it? How would you define it?

8. If your sex life and sexual confidence never changed or evolved for the rest of your life, would you be happy with the pleasure you currently experience? What changes would you make right now?

9. What do foreplay and aftercare mean to you? What do the lead-up to sex and behaviours after it has concluded look like and feel like in your fantasy? Now, why is it only a fantasy?

10. Make a list of the things you know about sex now that you wish you were taught as an adolescent. Write them

all down. These are no longer taboo for you; this is now an opportunity to help someone in your life have a better experience than you may have had when making your sexual debut.

taboo 4:

✖

The Sex You Didn't Want to Have

Late last year, I was privileged to host the Sydney launch of my friend Chanel Contos's book, *Consent Laid Bare*. Chanel is a trailblazer in consent education, and her book flattens patriarchy within the first fifty pages. It is a guide to ending rape culture. When I was interviewing her onstage at the University of New South Wales Roundhouse, one key line of Chanel's played on repeat in my mind. It is a quote that would go on to be plastered in the media in the weeks that followed:

'Women I know don't want to have sex like men.'

It healed a scab that I had been picking at within myself

for years. That not liking hookup culture did not make me less of a progressive woman, but just placed me in opposition to the kind of sex patriarchy wanted me to have. The sexual empowerment of women has been framed around us engaging in sex like men – which is not to say women *can't* like this, but that we haven't 'fixed' anything by encouraging women to have the 'sexual liberation' of men, with rape culture and slut shaming still intact. I believe it instead compelled us to accept our own dissatisfaction or, worse, violation. Sex positivity has been most open-heartedly adopted by our generation, but without the education and therefore sexual and emotional intelligence to match.

Generation Z are having less sex than ever before. A United States study of 2000 adults conducted by the Kinsey Institute and sex-toy company Lovehoney found that a quarter of gen Z adults say they have yet to have partnered sex. Interestingly, the report also found gen Z to be the 'kinkiest' generation. Young people are the most likely to report fantasising about sexual kinks including BDSM and are the most likely to say they have tried it in real life. While we're having less sex, the sex we are having is different from that had by the generations that precede us. We are also redefining what it means to have sex, applying different value judgements to what classifies as a sexual experience. La Trobe University findings say 60 per cent of young people consider oral sex to be sex, while 41 per cent believe the act of rubbing genitalia meets the definition of sex.

The LGBTQIA+ community inherently has a more expansive understanding and view of sex, compared to heterosexual people. We are challenging the narrative that penetration defines having a sexual experience. But make no mistake: this reduction in having partnered sex isn't because we are simply electing to rewrite the narrative of sexual empowerment – it is far more complex.

The Lovehoney and Kinsey Institute research determined a number of factors that led to the delay of our sexual debuts. Compared with millennials and gen X, gen Z adults reported the highest levels of stress and anxiety. Young adults reported a decline in sexual activity when experiencing these conditions. From COVID-19 to the cost-of-living crisis, it's no wonder younger adults are feeling the pressure at higher rates.

The US study also notably found that the retraction of reproductive rights was a significant factor in declining frequency of sex. One in five women reported feeling afraid to have sexual intercourse in the wake of *Roe v. Wade* being overturned, while 68 per cent were afraid it would negatively impact their capacity to experience pleasurable partnered sex.

Most corporations aren't catching on. In April 2024 Bumble, an app marketed as empowering women, launched a marketing campaign by erecting billboards in New York City shaming women who chose not to have sex. As *Time* reported in its coverage of the failed campaign, 'Bumble apologizes after getting stung for anti-celibacy campaign'. The publicly listed company backtracked and retracted signage that had said: 'You know full well a vow of celibacy is not the answer' juxtaposed against an introduction to 'the new Bumble'. Ironically, the updated campaign aimed to attract more generation Z women to the dating app. According to *Time*, Bumble's stocks have decreased in value since July 2023, dropping approximately 45 per cent in less than a year. It is directly linked to the dip in engagement with young people.

In a changing dating landscape, where generation Z, compared to millennials and generation X, reported the lowest level of interest in casual hookups and the highest investment in pursuing long-term relationships, the choice not to have sex is an emerging response to a rape culture under patriarchy that does not empower free choice over our own bodies or sexual experiences. We no longer want to be sold the lie that simply having sex is freedom. Instead, we want to be supported in the pursuit of pleasure. As Naomi Wolf wrote in 1990, 'We are being sold our own dissatisfaction. What is being advertised is a cure to self-hatred, the greatest trick is that it will solve nothing – you will just come back, wallet open, ready for more.' (It is important to note that while *The Beauty Myth* is a seminal text that provided groundbreaking insights into image and patriarchy, Wolf herself is now a conspiracy theorist with dangerous ideas. Her early work changed lives, but it is referenced in isolation from her current views.) In *The Beauty Myth*, Wolf writes:

The last thing the consumer index wants men and women to do is to figure out how to love one another: The $1.5 trillion retail-sales industry depends on sexual estrangement between men and women and is fuelled by sexual dissatisfaction. Ads do not sell sex – that would be counterproductive, if it meant that heterosexual women and men turned to one another and were gratified. What they sell is sexual discontent … What editors are obliged to appear to say that men want from women is actually what their advertisers want from women.

At the time this next story took place, I had not had sex in more than a year. I didn't desire having sex, but as I've said, this made me feel like I was failing as a young woman. I was struggling not to feel shame that I didn't want or need sex. I worried more that I had forgotten what to do – that I wouldn't be 'good' when I eventually did have sex again. I set myself the goal of going on two dates before Christmas.

My first date was one of the best I've ever been on. We went to a bar, then a bookstore, then a restaurant just for dessert. Seven or eight cocktails in, we went back to my house and had consensual sex. He set his alarm for 4am to go to work the next morning. I found it revolting that I was going to be subjected to that. The margaritas ensured I didn't care *that* much. We passed out.

But when the alarm went off, I felt his fingers start to find their way inside me. Without warning, without lube, without anything.

They stung.

My inner voice told me to stop tensing, but how could I tell my body to stop protecting me from something that made me feel unsafe?

What I needed was to be asked, but there had been no indication sex was going to be initiated. There had been no kiss, no touch of my back or my thigh. I'd used no body language to indicate I was aware of him or my surroundings. There was just his one swift movement. No communication. I often think, did he even check my facial expression? Whether my eyes were open?

I feel unsteady talking about this experience. I feel I was complicit. I struggle to label it as anything other than sex. I liked this guy; he had been gentle and sensitive and caring up to that point. More than anything, I was confused that his words and behaviours the previous night had not translated to this moment. I firmly believe that he just wanted to be dominant and initiate sex in the morning, that he didn't mean harm, but I wonder if I tell myself that because the truth is harder to stomach.

Within minutes it was all over. He asked if he should call in sick to work to spend the day with me; I said no. He said he would come back straight after his shift to make me dinner. I said, 'Sure,' and told him he was going to be late. It was still dark out, and I lay as still as I could under the covers – eyes closed. He wouldn't leave, planting kisses on unmoving lips. Eventually, the door closed behind him and I rolled over, putting a story on Close Friends Instagram to announce that I had broken my 'dry spell'. Looking back, I had not acknowledged or processed anything that had just occurred. I was frozen. I lay there for two hours and didn't sleep a wink.

When put in these positions, I wonder how often I have 'gone along' with sex to make myself feel like I made the choice. To feel in control. The alternative is to say no, and that presents a range of risks to my safety far worse than just 'tolerating'. But how could I psychologically process this experience? In a social climate in which survivors are not believed, what does it mean when I do not believe myself? When I make an experience of subjugation one of consensual sex in my mind?

These are the truths I believe exist all at once:

I didn't want to have sex.

He wanted to have sex.

He didn't seek my consent.

I didn't give consent.

Silence isn't consent.

We had sex.

I do not feel I can say nor do I believe I was sexually assaulted.

By criminal definition in most Australian jurisdictions, I was sexually assaulted.

He was not evil.

I am not a failed feminist for not saying anything.

I went along with it to ensure it ended faster.

I felt it was more uncomfortable and risky to stop him than to 'endure' it.

He was performing the kind of sex men think women want.

He should have talked to me about it. I believe he would have stopped if I had said something.

I will never know that for sure.

I regret not stopping him. I do not think he is a rapist.

I did not do anything about it.

I will never stop judging myself for not doing anything about it.

In the days afterwards, I had not contemplated any of the above. I was just pleased he had left my apartment. I had got over my sexual fear. In my mind, I had experienced intimacy again. I was ignoring the lingering feeling of discomfort sitting high up in my belly. I often fail to identify where my emotions are in my body in therapy, instead intellectualising every thought and feeling. I cancelled dinner.

He texted over and over and over again. I cancelled our plans, coming up with excuse after excuse as to why I could not see him. He would send fifteen text messages at a time, replying instantly to anything I said. I was frightened by his intensity. Eventually, I communicated that he was too overwhelming for me and that I didn't want to see him again. He apologised and told me to contact him if I changed my mind. I never did. He tried to reach out again, after he posted thirty-two heartbreak posts, and images and stories on his Instagram over the next five days. I blocked him and triple checked that my front door was locked every night that week. I asked my publisher to check the guest list at an upcoming book event to ensure he had not purchased a ticket. Only a week later when my best friend asked if he had kept contacting me did I say what had happened the morning after our date.

'You should tell him what he did.'

My leg is tapping under the table just recalling it.

'He will not do it to someone else if you talk to him. This is the kind of person who would benefit from that conversation.'

She was absolutely right. I was also right to not want to. I often wonder how many other women will be affected by my not saying something. I still feel like shit about that. Maybe writing it in this book is my way of rectifying that, for more men than just one.

The next man I had sex with put his hand around my throat the second I lay down on the bed. He strangled me multiple times during sex. I gently grabbed his arm to redirect him. Within ten minutes, it was back there. He looked down at me, so visibly confident that this decision was hot.

'What did you do the second time?' I hear you ask.

I did nothing.

'What did you say?' is an obvious next question I would

ask of me, because I never tend to treat myself in a sensitive, trauma-informed way.

I said nothing. I didn't stop him. I didn't stop having sex with him. I woke up in the morning and avoided seven of his sexual advances. I declined breakfast. I declined coffee. I drove home and I ghosted him. I then felt bad for ghosting him.

That's the worst part. I spend every single day talking to people about how to advocate for themselves, how to articulate complex thoughts and feelings and topics in simple and effective ways. I am a communicator. In my everyday life, I have quite literally almost never shut the fuck up, ever. Yet I was silent.

I am woven from the fabric of the social conditioning that I vocally, publicly work to tear apart in strips. There is so much I am yet to unlearn. Why can I post Instagram tiles in protest of sexual violence to my feed every single day, but stare at the ceiling when he places his hand around my neck? How can I claim to have a powerful voice when I do not use mine to stop him when it hurts? When violence is committed against me?

In these moments, I become obsessed with ridiculing myself and understanding and empathising with the other party. This is actually just control in overdrive. If I can get inside their head, if I can conceptualise and hack why they hurt me, the pain will be eased. Have you ever stopped to consider why you do not understand another person's behaviour? Perhaps it is because you would never treat someone the way you were just treated? My lack of understanding someone's poor behaviour is in fact a miracle – because I do not want to understand. I do not want to have that frame of reference. My obsession with understanding should not stand in place of my anger; it should not mean I learn to tolerate my own hurt. No one is going to give you a prize for anaesthetising yourself from someone else's behaviour towards you, for doing moral backflips until you find a way to blame yourself instead. If your best friend had the experience you're currently having, what would you say to her? If your son treated someone the way a sexual partner treated you, would you be proud of the person you raised?

Sometimes I watch my own videos back on Instagram, and the feminist messaging around sex and politics is so much stronger than how I feel in my day-to-day life. Most days I want to be more her, that version, than me. Does that sound ridiculous? The public projection of what I believe, what I want for all women, is more powerful and strong than the care with which I treat myself. It feels fraudulent, but I know it exists within all of us. We want better for our friends, our sisters, our colleagues, than we actually expect for ourselves.

These men I had sex with knew my work. They all had looked up Cheek before I went on dates with them. If men are willing to strangle me, to penetrate me without consent, having watched my content and read my books on the subject of women's rights – how deep does their entitlement run? How extreme is their cognitive dissonance? The belief of how men are supposed to perform sex, learned from porn, has eroded their perception of sex as an intimate act connecting two people. Either that, or they actively wanted to hurt me. I look around at the women in my life who do not openly talk about sex, who have not been as outspoken and who are not as progressive in their feminism. If the loudest, most privileged in the room are silenced, what does that mean for the quietest? What does that mean for the most vulnerable?

My fear is that most women are tolerating their heterosexual partnered experiences. That we have not been given the tools or the language to confidently ask for more from our male partners. That generations of older women endure, tolerate and dissociate to keep their husbands happy.

Men kill us. Men rape us. Men scream at us in the street, most often when we're wearing our school uniforms. We are told that just having sex with our partner who doesn't pay attention to us 'isn't that bad'.

He watches hardcore porn every day, where women are choked and hit. You feel it is your fault he cannot maintain an erection when you have sex.

The guy from your university college just showed a woman's nude to his mate over a beer. The friend glances quickly and then looks away, uncomfortable, but he politely chuckles during the commentary about her 'tits'. He does not say anything. The guy will do it again.

Your boyfriend skips your Instagram story about the Voice to Parliament referendum. He votes no because his mum says it is racist to white people. He shares a post of his favourite athlete's retirement announcement the next day. He's a great guy: your dad loves him. He also expects sex twice a day and doesn't really care if you don't want to. You're pressured into a yes, which isn't a yes at all.

Men look at you on the street, not with a friendly smile but as if you were crafted only for them. The lens through which they watch you on a Thursday afternoon as you head home from work has no care for your discomfort, because the only thing that matters is their desperation to degrade you with their eyes.

I often wonder when it starts for girls. What we watch, what we learn from the interactions around us that imposes the worldview from birth that we are accomplished as long as we are pleasing and available to men.

When I experience solo pleasure, I'm most often imagining. It is called 'mental framing', and research shows more than 90 per cent of women use it. Essentially, it is when you conjure a scenario to turn yourself on. This is where I find it easiest to understand the distinction between what women want during partnered sex and what men do not understand. It is a helpful tool in learning more about your own pleasure and bridging the gap between what you want from sex and what you actually experience.

The thought of penetration with a penis is one of the last things I'm conjuring in these moments. Not because I do not enjoy it, but because this is a reductive view of the mental act of partnered intercourse. If you were on Tumblr in 2012, you do not need to be told twice. I wish it was popular for men to read smut, because globally sex lives would improve. What I imagine is the slow touch of the back of my thigh. The way someone looks at me during sex, because they want to be having sex with me – not my body. I think of flirting at a dinner party, knowing you're going to leave the large gathering of people just to connect with each other. I think of tension and build-up and context. I'm never fantasising about being fingered by surprise at 4am. I don't ever imagine being strangled or hit by a partner I want to feel connected to. At the end of the day, is it 'vanilla' to have emotional sex? I want to explore different sexual dynamics and experiences – but without consent and the safety of a separate, controlled, respectful space for these sexual experiences to be tried, I'm not drawn to imagining them during solo pleasure.

In an earlier version of this chapter, I wrote that the man who put his hand around my throat choked me. I think I initially wrote 'choked' rather than 'strangled' to soften the act and use the language of porn, of kink. But the reality is that he took control of my airway and gave himself the power to end my life while he was inside me, without so much as asking. Imagine if I had said that to him. Imagine if I had said that at least three men I've had sex with have done the same thing. That each time, I had felt myself leave the experience altogether. I can feel myself dissociate during sex: it is one of the most disconnected and dehumanising experiences of all. When I dissociate I'm completely detached from what is happening in the room. I'm moving far, far away to another dimension where men look at me for the person I am, rather than as a pornographic vessel to test different acts on. The man who strangled me may have just thought I would find it hot; it may just be etched into his mind as acceptable, even needed, through watching violent videos. But what if it was just that he liked it? Inflicting violence on me? What did that mean? It seems simple enough to pass it off as 'porn teaching young men dangerous things', but what does each puzzle piece look like when you hold it up to the light? That men do not even have the foresight to consider that what they are doing is an act of violence? That they are not just doing something they are copying from a video, but that they find it pleasurable to threaten to take our lives?

In a 2023 article titled 'Sexual choking is now so common that many young people do not think it even requires consent. That's a problem' published in *The Guardian*, Chanel Contos wrote:

Another US study found that 58% of female college students have been choked during sex, further suggesting that this 'kink' is becoming increasingly common in younger age demographics. This study found that while many women enjoyed choking, others did it largely to please their sexual partner. This is the real kicker. The problem here is not only that women are being choked during sex without giving consent, but that a lot of the time they are 'consenting' not because they derive their own sexual pleasure from it, but because they think it turns the guy on.

Separating true consent from the desire to give your male partner sexual satisfaction is difficult. But I suggest that a good place to start is to equip young girls and women, who have grown up in an era where pornography has shaped every inch of their sexual landscape, with the capabilities to decide if it is an act they truly want to engage in.

I used to think I liked it. I've never once asked for it, but I firmly believed it was pleasurable dominance. Now, I understand that the submission I gain pleasure from is simply having someone guide me through intimacy, making decisions and working hard to pleasure me. I want to feel in the bedroom what I do not in other aspects of my life, that I do not have to be in charge. That still comes with trust, respect and consent. I do not throw those things out the window when I say feminists like submissive sex. Violence is not dominance.

The tail end of the millennial experience, one I grew up understanding as an elder member of generation Z, encompassed the narrative that heterosexual women had bad sex. This was a staple theme in popular culture during my teens and early twenties. Our current literary trends continue to reflect this obsession with shallow and unsatisfying sexual connections. The 'sad-girl novel' – fiction defined by depressed, anxious, hungover women who have reckless, bad sex with men in jobs they hate – is one of the most popular fiction categories. Sally Rooney, Meg Mason, Jessie Tu and Madeleine Grey are just a few of the prominent authors behind this literary phenomena. Sad girls are moody, complex and subvert the 'girlboss' by dissociating from everything that could create meaning in their life.

To me, they reflect a sexual revolution, led by online messaging, that showed us the unlimited forms of suffering in the world and invited us to find progress and escapism through the ability to have sex as frequently as we wanted and as unhappily as we could. The reality of these depictions is still steeped in choice feminism narratives that do not actually challenge patriarchy or dismantle taboo, but seek to validate the anguish of privileged cisgender white women. I believe gen Z women are sick of the victimhood of it all: we want sex to look different. The sad-girl novel captured the reality of many women's sexual experiences, but where can we go next? Can portrayals of heterosexual sex return to depicting genuine enjoyment?

My experience says so. Now, sex looks very different for me. It took reading Dr Emily Nagoski's books to understand that it was not that I had a low sex drive, that I was complicit in my own harm or that something was 'wrong with me', but that there were many 'brakes' in my life, my work, and my relationship and discomfort with sex that acted as barriers to pleasure and an active will and want to be touched, to be vulnerable and to be an enthusiastic participant in partnered sex. In her book *Come Together*, Dr Nagoski delivers the three characteristics of partnerships that sustain a strong sexual connection:

- They are friends – or, to put it more precisely, they trust and admire each other.
- They prioritise sex – that is, they decide that it matters for their relationship.
- Instead of accepting other people's opinions about how they are supposed to do sex in their partnership, they prioritise what's genuinely true for them and what works in their unique relationship.

And what do they do, these friends who prioritise sex and each other over any prefabricated notions of what sex is supposed to be? They co-create a context that makes it easier to access pleasure. That's it.

The first time I had sex with my current partner, I orgasmed and he didn't. 'A win for gender equality,' I joked the next morning over bacon and egg rolls. I'm really glad we basically started dating then and there because that joke could have really flopped. When I landed in a sexually satisfying relationship after consistently disconnected experiences, I felt lucky. That in itself feels revolting to articulate. I hadn't known satisfaction was possible until I found myself with a partner who required no teaching or redirecting but who nevertheless actively sought feedback and conversation. I felt safe, seen and prioritised. I had experienced good sex before, which is vital to acknowledge – I have had multiple kind men focus on my pleasure throughout my sexual history. But this was the first time in my life that I felt truly able to be with someone who matches the interest I express in sex and engages in the right (for me) dialogue about it. Who is learning to pick up every cue and is as happy to hear a 'no' as a 'yes'. 'Great, that means we can go for a walk to get a coffee together instead,' was genuinely the line I got when I didn't feel like it after a big breakfast on our second date. I love him, but this should be the baseline experience for all people when having partnered sex.

The pivotal moment for me, though, was during one of our first sexual experiences, when my vaginismus reared its head and I pretended not to be in pain. I didn't move my body, careful to remain in the same position, and just prayed it would end soon. I reverted to the old me, the silent woman who endured. I performed this role for less than three seconds.

'Hey, are you okay? I can tell you're not comfortable.'

Was it that obvious?

'I'm okay – we can keep going. I'm just in a bit of pain at this angle. I don't think I'm quite ready.'

'No, we aren't going to keep doing that. Let's stop. Can I do anything for you to help?'

It brought into sharp focus that this man did not want to *have sex*, he wanted to *have sex with me as an enthusiastic participant*. It sounds silly, but it was the distinction I needed. It was a gap that hadn't occurred to me before, as simple as it is. For him to know so swiftly that I had moved from pleasure to mere participation was proof of his constant attention to my wants, needs and active enjoyment. Since that day, I haven't seen or heard from my vaginismus. She might come back, and I'll welcome her with open arms ready to see how I can help.

Amid all the grey, I want to argue that heterosexual women do not have a dark future of dry vaginas and left flap rubs ahead of us. We know this because we are having great sex with ourselves – and now that I know how to channel that into partnered experiences, I'll never stare at the ceiling again.

if you could write a letter to men who have sex with the women you love, what would you tell them?

Hello, people I hope are hot, politically progressive and great with their hands,

I'd like to start by saying: lucky you. My friends are beautiful, kind and the right kind of critical. I pray you get this right for all our sakes. I will hear about it either way in excruciating detail.

I'm glad more men know where the clitoris is after years of social media pressuring you into caring about it.

Many of my friends have sex with people who are not men, and if this is you, there's no need to continue reading.

Back to it. I'd next like to suggest that you ask someone for feedback on how you're rubbing the clit. Just a thought: do not get confident with identification alone. We are not looking to have a fire started in our sacred areas, so let's get excited to learn more. Let's go beyond a couple of swipes before entry.

Now, I'm going to attempt to undo the learnings from the hardcore, violent pornography you've been watching to learn how to have sex. I can say pretty generally that we aren't liking that. Some people do, but until such a preference is explicitly confirmed, please do not hit us. We also do not like you thrashing around in the penetration department as if we are a mannequin for your needs. The jackhammer days are over. Unless we communicate clearly and directly that's what we want, it is not the default.

It isn't your fault that you thought all that was normal: we were also taught that was how it's supposed to be done. This might surprise you, but we were exposed to a lot of the same material. And now I'm telling you it isn't the way we like it to happen, so listen up.

First things first. Great sex is never *actually* about the sex.

Being 'good' at sex isn't about some very secretive coveted sex technique: it is about communication.

Sex is a mental act more than a physical one. Sexual 'skill' isn't all about placing a pillow under our lower back during penetration – although it does help a lot and I recommend you try it – it 's about emotional awareness. When we have sex, it can be sexy to say you want to 'fuck' us. But it's important to understand that sex isn't something you are doing to us. Your ability to pleasure a partner is directly related to your willingness to listen, to consider and to respond to their needs and wants. It is a rhythm you are moving to, a piece you are composing together. We are people constructing an experience that feeds on and improves with a constant feedback loop. It isn't sexually conservative or regressive to ask that we all start at a point of mutual respect, communication and seeing each other as equal partners with an equal share of needs, desires and wants.

We want to know about what you like just as much, but that involves you exploring yourself outside what the theatrics of mainstream porn have wrongly taught you. If you build to an understanding of power dynamics, kinks and curiosity — fantastic. I don't want to yuck your yum. I'm asking that you never assume. Sex is a mental act because it relies on individual interests and emotions: the connection is dependent on every person's psychological state and capacity to engage. Remember this every single time. Context is key.

Oh, this might just be almost every experience I've ever had, but please stop sticking your tongue down their throat. This is an important one. We aren't having a race to see who can imitate a washing machine fastest. Kiss on the lips, gently, and build to a more passionate open-mouth situation. Once again, I'm not claiming to have a one-size-fits-all answer here. But let connection evolve through pacing, feeling, responding. You need to check in and you need to be aware of your surroundings and your partner's the entire time. Do not rush — the momentum is the moment.

Penetration isn't an inevitability, but a potential pathway on an exploration of pleasure. Intimacy is not finalised through your orgasm; that is merely a part of the experience that can bring satisfaction to all people involved. It is attractive to ask, to check in, to improve. If you're struggling with an erection, please do not be anxious. A safe sexual partner will reassure you – we just want to know how we can help and talk it through with you. I feel closer to a sexual partner when they are willing to share these obstacles with me. It does not kill the vibe – it's a different opportunity for intimacy. Sex does not depend on your dick being hard. Have a shower, touch, cuddle, kiss, ask to go down on your partner, order a sweet treat. There are endless options.

Do ask them what you can do for them: verbally seeking feedback and instruction isn't 'ruining the mood'; it is bringing me closer to orgasm. It is showing me you care. Women feel more able to climax, more willing to release and experience pleasure for prolonged periods, when we feel safe to be in our bodies. Tell us we look beautiful; say we are hot. Affirm us. Seek and expect those same compliments and support in return from your partner. Words matter, and body language is vital. It is incredibly hot to be talked to during sex. Make noises, suggest things, look us in the eyes. Direct communication like this is attractive.

Foreplay and aftercare are not accessories to penetration; they are the main sexual events. If you are in a relationship, every single thing you do in the lead-up to sex is foreplay. The way you look at them when you wake up together. What you say as you're walking out the door. The dinner you planned for them tonight. The washing you did just to get ahead because you know they have a busy week. Did you get the crossword for them out of the paper (I am ninety years old; this is niche)? Are you capable of managing the household when they are having a tough day? Is this equal? Not in the 'I vacuumed two weeks ago though!' way, but in a genuine mental load way? It's in the way you text them throughout the day; how you talk about them with your friends and in front of your families; the things you do for yourself and your own mental health. Your consistency can define your connection. These are all central tenets of foreplay. We can feel desirable when we feel seen, heard and cared for. It isn't clothes off, a kiss on the mouth and a dick inside. It is our entire personhood. See us.

Aftercare is the post-sex ritual people engage in together. It is an opportunity to make sure every person feels safe, comfortable and cared for in whatever way they may need. Aftercare is the shower you have together. It is hand-holding and touch. Sometimes it is saving up the funny videos you've seen you know they would like. It is laughter and playfulness and cuddling. It is trip-planning and cocktail-making and candle-lighting. It is the clear understanding that you were not just seeking out sex, someone to get you off, but a connected experience with sexual partners you care for as people.

At all of the times in my life that I believed my libido

was 'low' or even 'dead', it was never because I didn't want to have sex – but because I didn't have sexual experiences that were intimate. I more often felt violated afterwards than connected. When we are struggling with low sex drive, do not suggest more sex. Look at the context in which sex exists; look at the factors impacting your and their mental health and lifestyle. Relinquish your expectations around sex entirely and make an effort to enjoy their company again. Carrying the mental load and caring for them in ways they appreciate and need are some of the most effective ways to identify why a disconnect has occurred and to turn back to one another.

One of the most important things you can do to improve partnered sex is this: consider what makes it easier for you to access pleasure. Go beyond penetration. What does your partner do that makes you feel attractive? What do you do for yourself that makes you feel desirable? What parts of sex make you feel best, and why? When you consider your authentic sexual self, not the performance derived from pornography or what you believe a man should be in the bedroom, you allow yourself to experience true intimacy.

You have been taught that your masculinity defines you, that the greatest shame is to be weak. But what if the self-belief that masculinity is the only option for men is part of that problem? Dating apps, hookup culture and situationships are all the result of a society of people scared of being alone or being in a long-term unhappy partnership. We need to take this insecurity and turn it into clear communication. Be the people you say you are, do not play games and always try to respond to your partners' bids for connection. When you're confused: ask. Sex, consent and intimacy are complex topics that we were never taught adequately. That will change for the next generation, but for now, ask the question. Most men are so afraid of getting it wrong that they never try to get it right, opting for silence or presumptions in place of clear conversation. We would prefer a partner who was clunky in their approach to consent to one who didn't ask. I would always choose someone who asks for feedback on their fingering over a confident man who hasn't made it past my labium majus for the last twenty minutes.

Feminist sex does not look like any one thing: it involves consenting parties who have an ongoing connection and discussion around their needs, their environment and their relationship with pleasure. As illustrator Flo Perry said in an interview with **Vice**, the most feminist sex people can have is the sex they want to have, not the sex they believe they should be having.

Oh, and lingerie is a gift for you. Not them. So buy it, but don't expect gratitude. It's a fun extra, not the centrepiece of a birthday or Christmas present (unless explicitly requested).

Also, please try reading smut instead of watching PornHub.

Hannah

3

relationships

Love is at the root of everything.
All learning, all parenting, all relationships.
Love or the lack of it.

Fred Rogers

questions to ask yourself about your relationship

- When you disagree, is it respectful? Do you feel heard?
- Are your politics 'different' or do they not see you as an equal human being?
- Do you actually like them or does it just feel familiar because that's how your dad treated you and your mum?
- Is this the relationship you'd want for your daughter?
- What about being single scares you?
- If nothing ever changed, would you be happy?
- Do you communicate your problems clearly?
- Do you communicate your love clearly?
- How would they react if asked to go to therapy?
- Do you feel loved? Do you feel known?
- What are you not telling your friends about the relationship?
- What do you talk about when no one else is around?
- Do they challenge you? How?
- Besides sex, how do you practise intimacy?
- Who have you become in this relationship?
- What would they need to do in order for you to leave?
- What would they need to do for you to want to stay forever?

taboo 5:

✗

Poor, Sad Single Women and the Future of Feminist Dating

The week before this book was due to my publisher, I spoke at the Sydney leg of the national rallies to end gender-based violence. I was having the kind of stomach cramps and accompanying gurgly tummy noises that indicate four nervous poos have all-aboarded the intestinal train. Unfortunately, I was standing behind a wall of cameras and microphones, praying the poos' estimated time of arrival at the back door of my body was not the exact moment I was expected in front of the crowd.

I'd had two panic attacks in my bedroom in the days leading up to the march. In my mind, it was not my place to speak and not my space to occupy. I was so terrified that I didn't prepare notes, panicking every time I sat down to jot down some reference points. I knew that anything that came out of me would be purely because of adrenaline, because of how I felt in that environment and what I could offer in that exact moment. Tens of thousands of women and hundreds of men marched through the Sydney CBD to demand a seismic, immediate change in understanding of and governmental responses to sexual, domestic and family violence. The prevention of men's violence against women, in the eyes of the government, could occur with 'generational shifts' and 'changing attitudes'. If you scratch the surface of what that means, it is this: if you women keep demanding equality and we do absolutely nothing to help, future children *might* not grow into violent men who are entitled to commit these crimes against you.

On that sunny Saturday, light striking the fountain at the centre of our Hyde Park landing spot, I stood side by side with thousands of women to converse about the way violence impacted us. We listened to the parents of victims, we listened to the children of victims, we allowed compassionate and nuanced examination of the complexities of violence and of the mental health implications, and we showed empathy to the men who were brave enough to go against the grain of Australian male attitudes and stand with us as allies. Women and non-binary people took a men's problem and voiced every way we could solve it. Thousands stood in the cool air and dug through the layers of grief and trauma of men's violence. We examined a 'problem' that was raping us, assaulting us and killing us, and we peacefully asked for help to fix it.

By the time I got up to speak, my heart was pounding in my throat. What could I possibly say to these thousands of people that they did not already know? I looked out at the cameras up to my eyeballs, the microphones set-up to capture every moment of vulnerability. I was disgusted. I saw reporters from Channel 7 capturing content for the evening news, after funding the lifestyle of a rapist for two years prior. I was livid. I watched as journalists worked for interviews and imagery of women who were exhausted – so tired of talking to other women about an issue that has never been our fault or our responsibility to fix. I saw publications who had worked hard to protect perpetrators now wanting the fifteen-second vox pop that would land well in the 6pm time slot. The very outlets known for reinforcing the problem suddenly wanted to film the solution, because it was newsworthy.

It was newsworthy in part because, compared with minority women, white women protesting are more palatable. They draw more eyes and therefore provide larger profit margins to the faceless individuals behind the mastheads. Murdered white women get more clicks than murdered minority women. That is the truth of these outlets and their coverage. They are the gatekeepers of what is visible, what is celebrated, what is problematic, what is a policy to be changed, or a topic to be muzzled. As the sun went down and speaker after speaker relentlessly dove to the depths of who they are and described the things that had happened to them, I wanted to weep. This was fodder for the media. This was just another article on their front page that wouldn't bother to mention the men at fault. Women are the face of men's violence: there is no other way to look at it. While there has been a popular argument to avoid giving any attention to the male perpetrators of these crimes, I disagree. The ugly truth is that we have become so desensitised to murdered women on our screens that it softens and reshapes our perception of the crime. For the men who dehumanise women, images of the victims won't land. The naming of men behind murder will.

As I walked home that day, fatigued, I was suddenly back in my body. As the adrenaline passed and I came crashing down, I realised I had bled straight through my favourite pair of jeans. Standing out in the park for three hours, tensions high, I just hadn't even realised that I needed a pad. My cycle was now fewer than fifteen days total. I was so stressed, with a failing contraceptive and an overload of work, that I had not realised I was bleeding in a one-week-on, one-week-off pattern. This had been going on for months. I was so exhausted, so taken by the words and the emotions of the day, I didn't realise I was bleeding heavily, or at all. I barely had the energy to care. Walking home, I could only think of my desperate need to stand under a searing shower to scrub it all away before putting on my comfiest flannelette pyjamas (they were twelve bucks at Aldi and I cannot ever mention them without adding that). My best friends ordered burgers, we ate a whole tub of garlic dip before they arrived and I lay horizontally for as long as I could before writing this.

I know more about men's violence than I do about my own menstrual cycle. This has always been the case. I have a deeper understanding of rape legislation than I do of cervical screening tests. I know which one I've googled more times. I know it is more acceptable for men to punch on at the pub during a football game than it is for me to use the word 'discharge' in a social setting. Google can help locate Viagra within a 500-metre radius, but finding a doctor who takes my concerns about painful sex and periods seriously will take at least several years of enduring them.

I think about the fact that women cannot use 'toxic masculinity' to describe toxic masculinity, because we are told the fix isn't shaming men. I then think about how many women have been shamed into silence at the hands of a partner committing sexual and domestic violence against them. I think about how the media shames us for our bodies, and how governments try to control them. I think about why that does not attract the same criticism as our phrasing choices: because our bodily functions are taboo, because our pain makes men feel uncomfortable, so could we please do it quietly over there? We are to be seen and not heard – to such an extent that men liking women, being intrigued by our interests, wanting our company or aligning with our feminism is more socially taboo than the men who commit violence against us.

My dad messaged me the morning after the rally: he had seen the video of my speech on Instagram.

Great rally speech. PM material.

My dad is one of the people who I wanted to hear my message loudest. His feedback and response were important. As a large, masculine, stereotypically 'Australian' man, what did he take away? What sank in? He had listened, but had he understood? I didn't need agreement that domestic violence is an issue; I needed reflection on how he would respond to the call to action. When I was little, my dad was the person I looked up to most. He's a man people gravitate towards, a man who works harder than anyone I know. He's a man who was not good at being a husband for many years. He's a man who is continuously trying to be a better dad, who is becoming increasingly progressive and aware of how his past behaviour has impacted his relationships. My dad shows up. He has hard conversations with me and he has allowed me to publish the following story. When I discussed it with him in the process of writing this book it was the first time he was told what had happened. I think his allowing me to write about this is, in itself, the ultimate act of progress. He knows what it means to me to be able to share this with people. My parents make me believe every day that we are all capable of learning, of growing and of conversing with each other about hard things.

When I was eighteen, I returned from university in Brisbane during the semester break to my hometown in Orange, in central west New South Wales. My mum asked if I would come and meet the psychologist who had been seeing both my brother and sister. I thought that was a nice idea.

At the time, my parents were two years post separation and an Apprehended Violence Order was in place. This ensured my dad did not go within a certain distance of my mum. The AVO had been functional for almost the entire period since their split. Their separation, during my final year of school, was an incredibly stressful and traumatising time – especially for my brother and sister, who were only ten and twelve.

I had grown accustomed to receiving urgent phone calls from both Mum and Dad at different times throughout this stretch, one fearing for her own safety and the other with serious mental health concerns. Dad needed help, but Mum needed protection. I was trying to provide both, while also wanting to be far away from them. I was failing at all these attempts. I have not told many people in my life about what happened during this period, mostly because I feel it does not 'qualify' me as enough of a victim to give my story sufficient worth. I know this is absurd intellectually, but not emotionally. The other part is that I still speak to everyone in my family, and recalling this feels like a breach of their trust and our relationships. I want to make it clear: I love my parents, and this is a complex dynamic to carry. This is the truth from my personal perspective, and I do not claim it to match the truths of my relatives.

When I was sitting in the psychologist's office with my mum, she told me that she had brought me here to chat with her. At first I thought it was potentially for treatment, which I had been averse to. I gave a 'fine' look and nodded as we walked into the room together. The psychologist and my mum sat directly across from me. After a few minutes of general chatter, my siblings' psychologist offered me a glass of water and began the conversation – the real reason I was there.

'Hannah, you are staying in Orange until Wednesday – is that right?'

'Yeah. I have two birthday parties and a couple of people to catch up with,' I told her.

'And Max and Kate are travelling to stay with your dad in Queensland?'

'Yep, on Saturday. Is that right, Mum?'

'That's what we want to talk to you about.'

Mum looked at her shoes.

'Okay.'

'We have concerns your dad may attempt to hurt your brother and sister.'

The psychologist paused, looked straight into my eyes and took a breath before continuing. 'When violence and stalking behaviours are present, there is a heightened risk that he may hurt – kill – the children in order to get back at your mum. There are a few factors that can drastically reduce the likelihood of that occurring, and one is the presence of a guardian. You are much older than them, and he is far less likely to hurt you. My understanding is that he sees you as an adult, but not them. We believe it would be best if you go with them as a precautionary measure. You would be their guardian in these circumstances.'

I looked at Mum. My eyes were pleading and betrayed. I was eighteen. I felt overwhelmed by what was being placed on me and distressed about losing all the plans I had made and missing out on the time I got to spend at home by myself. I knew I was being selfish. 'Mum, that isn't going to happen. I have events to go to.'

'But imagine if it does happen … and you stayed behind.'

I think about this moment in my life a lot.

It is my belief that my dad would never do such a thing, but at the time, all I knew for sure was that he was as mentally unwell as he had ever been in his life. My father was experiencing significant suicidal ideation. He will be the first to admit that. I love my dad, and I trust my dad. We have a relationship that has grown and improved in the last few years. He engages with everything I do and he backs me, even when he disagrees.

Taboo

It was only three or four years later that I began to understand the psychological impact that conversation had on me. Something I had pushed aside as being an overly worried parent and a mental-health professional asking me to change my plans now resides at a much deeper level in my psyche. Seven years on, I have the emotional capacity to understand that I was truly being tasked with intervening in a double murder: the ultimate act of family violence. Whether there was actually any risk of it occurring is beside the point. When a young woman just reaching adulthood is faced with that kind of emotional strain, what does it teach her about relationships, violence and her own role within these dynamics?

During interviews and events, lots of strangers ask me how I came to be 'this person'. But who is 'this person'? Even contemplating that question makes me feel like an egotistical mole. How do I answer that? As an insecure twenty-five-year-old posing as a confident woman, I'm never sure what the truth is versus 'what I'm supposed to say'. Should I be honest, or is that unhelpful to women and 'the movement'? Should I say I'm insecure and that they would hate to hear what my psychologist has heard? Or should I smile and tell them to 'push through that imposter syndrome, queen!! You've got this!!'

I know innately that I've accumulated most of my skills and qualities because of my own passion and drive, and because of the people I love, from whom I learn different things. But too often I worry that much of who I am is because of the dark sharp parts, the bits that shouldn't have had to happen. Too often I associate my best qualities with the pain and trauma I've experienced. How do I reckon with that? Who could I have been without these spikes and edges? Why did an eighteen-year-old have to hold all of that? Why can I still not put any of it down? If I do put it down, will I lose the career I have built articulating all of this for an audience of people who identify with it?

When I spoke at the rally without preparation, I think it was this heavy weight in my stomach, all the things I've been carrying around, coming to the surface. I wanted to scream on behalf of those who couldn't any more. I wanted the changemakers to understand that they should not be walking beside us, because in fact they have been elected to walk three steps ahead and help bring us into a future free from these attitudes and behaviours. I wanted media decision-makers to know they were supposed to be two steps ahead, reporting to us and informing us. Instead, we're dragging them out of the victim-blaming of centuries past.

I worry that in many ways it is wrong of me to share thoughts like this, and I fear the response if my loved ones read what I've written. Ultimately, I hate that people think I'm confident in what I say and do. The idea people have that I do not feel fear or anxiety about the statements I make and the experiences I share is laughable. I am terrified and I am exhausted. I know most of us are. I never want to push someone to share something and ignore their discomfort, but I do want to shine light on the impact you can have when you push through these layers of anxiety and challenge the alienation we risk in speaking out. Courage is born of vulnerability. Acts of courage breed further courage.

I am tired of patriarchy's violence against women, but I'm just as tired of women believing it is our secret to keep and our problem to fix. I am tired of women sticking it out in relationships that 'are not that bad', because our default belief system is that a single woman is somehow sadder than an unhappily partnered one. I grew up around these conversations. I grew up leading these conversations with my baby brother and sister. When I started dating, I realised I hadn't had these talks with myself. How could I pursue a healthy relationship when what I feared most was becoming exactly like my mum and dad?

X

'Feminism has gone too far,' a man told me on a dating app last year.

It was his opening line, which was incredibly charming and transformed my vagina into a waterslide; I was just *desperate* to have sex with him. It was one of many sensual, romantic lines I had been presented with in the two years I had spent swiping in Australia's second-largest city in a year I had wrongly believed to be further progressed than 1912. Time after time, the same shit arrived under the photo of me smiling with my debut book, *Bite Back: Feminism, Media, Politics and Our Power to Change it All*: 'The gender pay gap isn't real,' 'Feminazi,' 'Does that mean I can hit you then,' 'You should be conscripted for war too,' 'You can pay for dinner,' 'I've always wanted to fuck someone taller than me.' This is just a sample of the top-notch shit I faced.

The rebuttal to be made is that these men are the night watchmen of patriarchy, not the majority. But it isn't a cohort of extremist incels who think this way: it's a significant portion of young adult men. It isn't due to a lack of education or awareness. Australian men hold some of the most misogynistic views in the Western world, according to 2022 data by research firm Ipsos and the Global Institute for Women's Leadership (GIWL). Their findings showed 32 per cent of Australian men agree that men have 'lost out' economically, politically and socially 'as a result of feminism'. In this global study, Australian men were the second-highest cohort to agree with the statement 'gender inequality does not really exist'. We came second to Saudi Arabia. Yep.

The extremism of straight white cis men is not seen as a radicalisation worthy of alarm in Western society. As I mentioned earlier, the term 'toxic masculinity' is now discouraged because experts in mental health and male violence say it shames men. I would argue that men's inability to cope with the language of accountability further proves and works to distort and conceal the problem. Women are being raped and murdered, and men want to be *coddled* into better behaviour. If we cannot use accurate language to describe the actions they engage in, does that conceal the reality of this epidemic? Men hate women, men hurt women, and women are not able to name this truth for fear of alienation or being seen as angry. Can we fucking hear ourselves? In an article published in *The Big Issue*, Everyday Sexism Project founder Laura Bates says 'If you look at the numbers, twelve million survivors of discrimination, harassment, assault and abuse shared their stories through #MeToo.' 'And *The New York Times* estimates that about 200 men faced any kind of repercussions as a result, the vast majority of them not even legal repercussions … This idea that the pendulum has swung a bit too far, that feminism has gone too far, and men are the victims now is complete nonsense.'

When a man opens a conversation on a dating app with, 'You'll do just fine', I'm less inclined to risk my safety and waste two hours of my Thursday night having a drink with him – knowing he won't remember my name and does not know how to use an iron. I would also prefer to avoid having to tell him my bank account looks a lot better than his when he eventually makes a comment about feminists having to pay equally on the first date. As a heterosexual woman, this is the landscape of dating men in 2024. Proof that sexuality is not a choice. There is not only a lack of profiles where men are pictured without sunglasses and eight beers in their hands, but also an active danger to our safety.

There is a commitment to misunderstanding what equal relationships ask of them, and what feminism asks of straight men more broadly. In her book *Invisible Women: Exposing Data Bias in a World Designed for Men*, Caroline Criado Perez writes:

> A man I briefly dated tried to win arguments with me by telling me I was blinded by ideology. I couldn't see the world objectively, he said, or rationally, because I was a feminist and I saw everything through feminist eyes. When I pointed out that this was true for him too (he identified as a libertarian) he demurred. No. That was just objective, common sense – de Beauvoir's 'absolute truth'. For him, the way he saw the world was universal, while feminism – seeing the world from a female perspective – was niche. Ideological.

I have carried the belief from a young age that most people, and I mean *most*, are in relationships they are unhappy in. For a long time I was told that was because my parents were unhappy together and my skew was bad. Then came Daniel Sloss. I watched his 2018 Netflix special *Jigsaw* with my best friend, Hayley, who is an expert in stand-up comedy. She knew I would love Sloss, because he does what very few white men in comedy can do – he melds dark humour with intellectual social commentary. *Jigsaw* ended more than 250,000 relationships. It ended so many that Sloss stopped counting: he has had hundreds of people ask him to sign their divorce papers.

He used his newfound fame from this special to talk about his best friend's rape, having introduced the perpetrator to her. Daniel Sloss is one of the men leading a conversation between men on sexual violence and abusive relationships. In *Jigsaw*, he writes a love letter to being single – by calling out the fact that most people have romanticised the idea of romance, and that this belief is cancerous. *Jigsaw* criticises the way our romantic lives have been made the centrepieces of our personal puzzles: we build around them and rarely stop to actually consider whether this centrepiece serves us. Often, resentments have to build over years in order for a breakup to occur. How many times have you seen someone you love wait for their partner to 'do something bad', like cheat, in order for them to feel justified in choosing to be single?

Commonly, men are 'shocked' and 'blindsided' by breakups. When I hear this, I find it hard not to interject with an 'I doubt it.' Because every woman I know has been sitting on her breakup for six months, withdrawing emotionally over a long period of time from a partner who hasn't provided her with what she needs, despite countless requests and careful articulations. When she leaves, he is suddenly overcome with emotion and loss, because her partner has lost one of his core emotional pillars. Too often, he's lost a mother figure he also expects sex from. That isn't an equal relationship; it is parasitic. To anyone reading this who is attracted to men, please know that it is normal to be turned off sex after you've had to show your boyfriend how to wipe his own arse properly. If he cannot prevent his own skid marks, buy the right laundry liquid at the shops or boil an egg, leave. You are not going to change someone by doing everything for them: you are going to have a child you didn't give birth to. I would rather be alone my entire life than mother a man society believes, and continues to tell me, is my protector. I'm six-foot-two and run my own company at the age of twenty-five: if I cannot come home to a partner capable of asking me about my day, cooking me a nice meal and providing consensual, connected sex, I'll stick to living with my friends and my vibrators. I do not just 'deserve' this because of those attributes; all people do.

From the moment we are born, girls quickly understand that the worst thing a woman can be is alone. By 'alone', we do not mean without community – just without a partner. Single women are considered un-maternal, troubled, difficult, scorned. We are angry and bitter and we hate men. But I do not hate men – I am romantically attracted to them. I dislike that women accept the bare minimum in order to be partnered (unhappily), and I dislike that men benefit from and lean into this – consciously or not. Being romantically untethered does not make single women alone; it means they only want people in their life who complement it. I believe being alone is necessary.

Taboo

We must know ourselves in order to know how we want to be loved. In *All About Love: New Visions*, bell hooks writes: 'Many of us seek community solely to escape the fear of being alone. Knowing how to be solitary is central to the art of loving. When we can be alone, we can be with others without using them as a means of escape.'

According to a study by Morgan Stanley, 45 per cent of women aged twenty-five to forty-four are expected to be single and childfree by 2030. In response to this statistic, author Farida D. wrote: 'Beware. The patriarchy will convince you that this is a terrible thing to happen to women. But it is in fact a terrible thing to happen to men.' The research backs her statement, with several studies indicating that the happiest women are both single and childfree. Paul Dolan, a professor of behavioural science at the London School of Economics, said during an infamous speech in 2019 that the evidence showed that the traditional markers used to measure success did not correlate with happiness:

> We do have some good longitudinal data following the same people over time, but I am going to do a massive disservice to that science and just say: if you are a man, you should probably get married; if you are a woman, do not bother ... You see a single woman of forty, who has never had children – 'Bless, that's a shame, isn't it? Maybe one day you'll meet the right guy and that'll

change.' No, maybe she'll meet the wrong guy and that'll change. Maybe she'll meet a guy who makes her less happy and healthy, and die sooner.

The day my debut book *Bite Back* was released was the biggest of my life. My family and friends came together to see me speak at a sold-out Sydney launch event. Red dress and heels, professional makeup and hair styling and two drinks deep, I was standing in the biggest moment of my career. I spoke well. I had already sold 3000 books in the first week of sales and I was vulnerable, anxious and trying to bolster my courage with that success. I was taking it all in. This was not something that usually happens for debut authors; this was not normal for a twenty-five-year-old. All my friends and family were gathered in one place, and no one fought. I was running on adrenaline and excitement, attempting to just feel the joy without thinking ahead, dreaming of what would come next. After the event, having dinner with my best friends at a pub four blocks down from the venue, I leaned across the table to one of my high-school friends.

'Can I look at your Instagram account for a second? I just need to check something.'

'Checking something' was actually looking at the private Instagram account of a woman I knew she was following. I suspected she was dating the guy I had been seeing the four months prior. He didn't like me enough to be in a relationship with me, but he wouldn't leave me alone, continually coming back into my life and leaving as he saw fit. I didn't understand this, so I excused it as an emotional struggle of his that I could 'fix'. I allowed him back in like clockwork.

Here I was, red wine in hand, after signing books and taking photographs with every person I loved, taking a break on my friend's phone to scour the private account of a woman who had posted a grid carousel of them together on holiday, a romantic overseas trip. I handed the phone back quickly to my friend, attempting to conceal from her what I had been browsing. She saw anyway, connecting the dots at a speed only best friends can. Her face dropped. I still wonder if she felt sad about my discovery, or sad that I had looked in the first place. I do not say this as a woman scorned or betrayed. I say it as a twenty-five-year-old feminist who, on the biggest day of her life, was determined to cause herself pain over a guy who did not care about her. My focus and attention was not on my loved ones or my significant achievement, but on a man who had been lying to me and betraying his apparent partner.

Each and every day, as Cheek followers sought endless advice on having conversations with their partners and how to set up a dating profile, I was dishing out insights I never put into practice. I believed others deserved better in their relationships, but I didn't in mine. It is no surprise to me why I was doing this, but I couldn't beat it. I can intellectualise the problem, having the awareness to understand the how and the why of my behaviour, but I lacked the connection to my body to actually sit with emotion, process my feelings and choose to change. I had been centring men in my life and preaching the exact opposite. I felt pathetic. I thought this made me a failed feminist, a progressive woman who was projecting a public image of empowerment and strength in independence and single life, while behind the scenes I was reading my horoscope for clues about my love life. I would watch tarot readers on TikTok tell me my dating experience was about to get MUCH better as soon as the moon eclipsed or phased or transcended something. Embarrassing, but it helped me get to sleep.

It was not about that particular man, though: that became clear. He was only evidence of a deeper problem. It was what he caused in me. His treatment of me caused me to leave myself – the self I know and love, my own trust and respect. When I let a man cut me off from my sense of self, I departed from the one person who will constantly be with me. Every time I responded to a text, every time I was drawn in again by someone who picked me up and discarded me as he saw fit, I betrayed myself. I do not want to normalise this. It isn't me saying, 'If you look up to me, don't worry – I let myself get treated like shit too!' It is to say that very few of us are actually able to rise above this conditioning: it takes years of awareness and practise to actually enact the belief system you project to the world.

While I was single, I found it easier to not engage in dating at all than to simply exist on the apps. I wanted clear lines:

Taboo

I was either content with no dating, sex or romantic pursuits of any kind, or I was meeting men with the clear goal of finding someone I wanted to pursue a long-term relationship with. I have never enjoyed casual, in-between or almost – not in my hobbies, work, friendships or partners. It may sound intense, but I like to be decisive about what I enjoy and how I give out my time and energy. Dating actively was the most anxiety-inducing experience of my life: constantly reviewing my own profile, feeling the rejection of the system of swiping, and engaging in surface-level connections over and over and over again in the hope of breaking through with a prospective partner. As someone with strong female friendships and a full work life, this was shaky middle ground that did not reflect the fullness of my life. I didn't need to meet new people – I was searching for something specific.

What do I want for myself? It isn't definitive. It isn't a long-term partner or children. It isn't marriage. What I want is to remain so aware of myself, so intelligent and so secure in my decisions that I am never trapped in believing I must conform to the conditions my mother and grandmother were forced to live in. I want the financial literacy to protect myself, I want to be challenging enough to demand more from a world that treats me as inferior, I want to always strive to know better. If that allows for a long-term partner who values me and the things I want for myself, fantastic.

Research tells us that neither men nor women are surviving

securely in the modern dating world. A US study conducted by Harvard's T.H. Chan School of Public Health found that women were particularly vulnerable, with those who use dating apps exhibiting 2.3 to 26.9 times higher odds of using elevated 'unhealthy weight control behaviours'. That includes self-induced vomiting, fasting or using diet pills and laxatives, which are all symptoms of eating disorders. Meanwhile, men who date online are also at greater risk, with 3.2 to 14.6 times the odds of using unhealthy weight management practices, including using steroids.

Dating is a vulnerable act for all, but it disproportionately places women at risk. In 2018, South Korean women started a radical feminist movement called 4B – short for four Korean words beginning with *bi*, meaning 'no'. The first is *bihon*, the rejection of heterosexual marriage, followed by *bichulsan*, the stance against childbirth, *biyeonae*, the refusal to date, and *bisekseu*, the rejection of heterosexual sexual relationships. A piece in *The Cut* explored the movement and its roots: 'A World Without Men: The women of South Korea's 4B movement aren't fighting the patriarchy – they're leaving it behind entirely.' Within the essay, Anna Louie Sussman writes that the movement itself began with the non-married women of the nation and expanded to a ban on reproductive labour.

In South Korea, 4B is an escape from the tightly imposed conditions of patriarchy that grew with the nation's spike in femicide, sexually violent crimes and a lack of legal accountability for the male perpetrators responsible. The trend is a smaller, more radical extension of the country's 'escape the corset' movement, which saw Korean women explicitly reject societal beauty standards by cutting their hair short and going barefaced. The data backs the scope of the movement, with a 2019 survey finding that 24 per cent of women in their twenties reported cutting back their spending on beauty products in the previous year. This is a notable time period, given that K-beauty grew in the United States market by 300 per cent between 2016 and 2018. As the Korean audience reduced their engagement with the beauty industry, it exploded in the West.

Sussman says that it is unclear how widespread or popular the 4B movement is given its fluid online and offline nature and its evolution over the years. One article approximated 50,000 followers, while others believe the movement to have less than 5000 adherents. However, there are significant statistics that indicate the shift in women's lifestyles. In 2016, Korea's fertility rate was 1.2 births per woman; it has since decreased to 0.78 – the lowest globally. *The Cut*'s piece sharply underscored the way systems of patriarchy respond to women's collective outrage by moving the blame to feminism and away from men's violence:

> The Korean government launched an online 'National Birth Map' that showed the number of women of reproductive age in each municipality, illustrating just what it expected of its female citizens. (South Korean

president Yoon Suk-yeol won the election in March 2022 with a message that blamed feminism for Korea's low birth rate, and a promise to abolish the country's Ministry of Gender Equality and Family.) Women were outraged by the map, observing that the government appeared to consider them 'livestock'; one Twitter user reportedly created a mock map illustrating the concentration of Korean men with sexual dysfunction. Several of these digital feminists responded with a boycott to the reproductive labor expected by the state and decided that the surest way to avoid pregnancy was to avoid men altogether. It was through these online communities that 4B emerged as a slogan, and ultimately a movement.

Yes, the movement is an extreme response, which also raises interesting questions around women's own sexuality – and the expectation to withdraw from engaging in romance, connection and partnered sex as a form of protest. I am not a proponent of the complete denial of dating, sex or having children, but the concept raises a striking point. If the greatest risk to a woman is being in a heterosexual relationship with a man, to refuse that risk makes sense, at least on paper. To instead actively choose to remain single and childfree, knowing that data tells us those women are happiest and live the longest, seems like a rational decision for single women to make. Men providing us with a safe, secure and equal relationship is the bare minimum. We live in a nation where 27 per cent of women have experienced violence or abuse from an intimate partner since the age of fifteen, according to the Australian Bureau of Statistics in 2023. We also live in a nation where, clearly, men do not believe in the equality of all people. Why should we provide intimacy, commitment, children or emotional and mental labour to men who see us as inferior?

The legal frameworks and social stigmas around divorce convinced women for most of history that they were possessed by either their fathers or their husbands, that long-term commitment to a relationship, even a bad one, was expected. Then, it was just considered admirable. The truth is, respecting yourself enough to leave is an act worthy of applause. For me the 4B movement highlights that, while it is not our fault when men treat us poorly, it is within our power to not accept bad behaviour. Noting, of course, that this does not apply to the experiences of victims of abuse or the conditioning that accompanies so many undermined people. But many of us do have the choice to stop having sex with people who do not like us. To stop convincing men to date us, to see us, to love us. To stop parenting a partner who knows you we available to serve them.

This behaviour is so normalised by women dating men that we consider it a fun brunch conversation. Women have defined a culture of gossip around all the things men have done to us. I've watched countless viral TikTok trends of women naming things their exes did to them and they stayed, stooping lower and lower each time, for 'comedy'. Taylor Swift, arguably the most commercially successful woman in the world, has built years of art around what men have done to her. At a certain point, is it not just sad that this is a never-ending source of content?

When I think about my private desperation to continue engaging with men who did not respect or care for me, it is because these toxic relationship dynamics were familiar: one-sided longing versus a brick wall. When this is the relationship you grow up inside, viewing it from every angle, this is the behaviour that is normalised. My earliest memories are of refereeing my parents' fights, so now my nervous system is more comfortable in conflict than in love.

I grew up in a household where love was not present between my parents. They didn't cuddle. They didn't kiss. They didn't touch. They were sometimes friends, but it was not equal. It was about power; it was about begging and grovelling to be heard. It was raised voices and empty living rooms because someone came home in a mood, and my presence in shared spaces meant I had positioned myself in the warpath of emotional dysregulation. You were hit for something today that yesterday you were praised for. They fought about the sex they didn't have in front of me. I watched my father tell my mother he would murder her and then kill himself if she cheated on him. He thought it was funny. I never once saw him get her flowers, tell her he loved her or do anything to make their marriage one worth staying in. He once told her she was hot when he was fifteen beers deep at a rugby game. She told me this excitedly eight times in the weeks that followed. When you are terrified that you'll end up in a relationship that mirrors your parents', there's a jolt when you are presented with a dynamic you've never experienced before.

One of the most interesting social scientists I follow, Katie Jgln, wrote a piece on Substack: 'Why Women Pay the Price for Caring for and Understanding Men: On the emotional and hermeneutic labour in romantic relationships and what it can cost us'. The article is essentially a philosophical exploration of inequality in the emotional labour of heterosexual relationships. Jgln cites philosophy professor Ellie Anderson, who argues an extension beyond emotional labour, coined 'hermeneutic labour'. This is where partners go beyond simply 'therapising' and into a more sophisticated layer of cognitive load and understanding that many women continue to work on in heterosexual relationships. Anderson advanced the concept after observing how much psychological work women tend to do interpreting the 'cues and scarce words' of their male romantic partners, who often lack the emotional vocabulary to explain themselves properly, and then imagining what they might be feeling or needing and carefully crafting their action plan in response. Jgln says:

As Anderson puts it, it is 'the entanglement of self and

other, as well as of cognition and emotion'. And just like emotional labour, hermeneutic labour is both demanded from women but also rendered largely invisible and hence undervalued.

I think of how often I have watched friends beg their partners to go to therapy, and how closely they monitor the mental and emotional health of their partners and the relationship more broadly. I then remember that society sees men as our protectors, but the reality is we are protecting them every single day. This is labour we are so used to performing we may not even notice ourselves doing it.

In 2023, after a long period of not engaging with any romantic prospects, I began a period of dating and having sex with people to learn more about my own intimate needs and what I was actually looking for in a prospective partner. I knew I had to push myself to meet lots of new people and try to find the fun in connection again. I went on seven first dates over the course of two months. Every date I went on lasted at least four hours. I was reminded that I was fun, that I was good at this. I carefully selected who I went on dates with, but I was more open than I had been previously to meeting people from different backgrounds, with different political views. I pushed myself, knowing that after fixating on someone who had the markers on paper of the partner I wanted and none of the actual qualities of a good man, I needed to put my ego and 'type' aside and start prioritising the experience. The approach I took was: be the person you'd want to date. Strip the fuck away from the gender norms our algorithms continue to shove down our throats and ask yourself what you want from your partner, feel comfortable accessing those parts of yourself and communicate accordingly. Could dating be about connection and fun, and not infected by anxious intrusive thoughts?

I started replying at the speed I wanted to, not on the basis of how they were replying. I asked men on dates, and then I asked them to plan the date to take the mental load off me. I paid the bill when I wanted to and I accepted them paying the bill too. I flew to Melbourne on a whim for a first date and booked work meetings around it. I became less concerned with how I 'performed' and looked on a date and more with how many questions they asked me and the substance of those questions. I asked if they'd been to therapy, how they voted in the referendum and what they think of their mothers, all on the first date. I made my dating profile more me. After a six-month period of no dating, I went from setting a midnight alarm to wake up and see if the guy had late-night texted me for sex to never organising dates on weekends to ensure my time with my friends was protected and well spent. I had reset my psychology around dating. I shifted from completely miserable dependency on swiping to wanting connection to be fun again.

Then enter: the group date. When I originally voiced the idea, I had no clue this would become one of the central aspects of my work and life for the next few months. It was inspired by a piece of content I had seen online: a TikTok about four single women, roommates, who each brought a first date over for a pasta night. None of the men knew what they were walking into: a group first date. Bottle of wine in hand, each new entrant was filmed entering in shock and then welcomed into the home.

The hypothesis hummed in the back of my mind for a while. I explained the idea on Instagram, expressing to my followers over a series of videos the concept laid out in the clip, and asking whether they thought it was feasible and what they would change. Thousands of responses poured in. Most people were concerned about consent. Of course, that was a given. The key ingredient to a functional group-dating experience was that all parties needed to know what they were stepping into. There were other obvious responses around the women's safety, the potential for what people described as 'partner swapping', and how to get to know someone in a social environment of that nature. All the insecurities and intricacies of modern dating were emerging exactly as I'd expected. They reflected our current social landscape: women's safety, men's egos and the offence of rejection in favour of another 'hotter' (or potentially just more compatible) person.

The first poll I conducted with my followers around the idea of a group date was to gauge their level of personal interest: 'Would you attend this type of group date if you were invited?' Of the more than 2000 respondents: 27 per cent said, 'yes – for a first date', 46 per cent said, 'yes – after meeting the date once before' and 27 per cent said, 'I would rather stick a rusty fork in my eye'. (Apologies, at the time I didn't consider that I might be citing my incredibly clever and funny Instagram content as data in my book.) After considering the responses, I walked downstairs to my two single roommates and best friends. We were all dating and we were all fatigued by the apps.

'How are the responses going?' my housemate Annie asked.

'The people have spoken,' I said, as if I were a reality-show host voting someone off the island. 'I think we should do it.'

Cue momentary silence and contemplation.

'*Can* we actually do this?' I asked again, bridging the gap between the giggly, fun idea and the reality of committing to and executing it. All my closest friends are introverted and want nothing to do with my online self, so I knew I was pushing some serious buttons here.

They agreed to the group event on the condition that I 'project managed' the experience. We settled on a date eight days away: the following Friday. Throughout the week I kept my followers updated on the planning and execution. I had quite a few people (mostly men) critique me, suggesting I was using the men we had invited for content, like guinea pigs. Despite me saying several times that we were building a consensual experience for a group date, people were concerned for the heterosexual men involved. They wanted to make sure they were not game-show contestants. They wanted to protect them from a 'social experiment', as if

I was performing a harmful exploitation for research. In the broader context of dating – where women send their friends location pins, screenshots of the guys' dating profiles and messages such as, *If I do not text you by 10pm I'm probably cut up into tiny pieces somewhere in a garbage bag – send help*, followed by a 'fit check' survey of multiple cute ensembles – I found it fascinating that so many men jumped into action to defend the honour of strangers, who they were worried I was hoodwinking by transparently inviting them over for a triple date.

Realistically, we as three women were more at risk in our own home than the men were, and yet spectating men jumped to the conclusion that somehow *our dates* were the victims of an act they were consenting to. What these people assumed was that I was going to secretly film the date or that my intention was to use them for content. Interesting, given my career is built on respectful, healthy relationships and conversations.

A week out from the date, we had each secured a man who was excited for the experience. Two were through Hinge, and the third was a guy I had been set up with by a mutual friend, who I thought would get along much better with one of my roommates. I expected that Hannah my-nickname-in-year-two-was-Shrek Ferguson was not going to be his preference.

Then, tragedy struck. On the Monday prior, my date pulled out. I panicked. I hadn't even made it to him choosing someone else. Now I was the one without the date – it was my idea and I couldn't even get someone there.

'Hannah, have you forgotten that you have a hundred thousand followers you can ask?' Lilli said.

Um, no? 'Hi, everyone, just so you know my date does not want to meet me any more so can one of you show up please? I'm pathetic and desperate.' I fell on the lounge, laying the back of my hand on my forehead as if the world were crashing down on me. It was. I required a hot cinnamon doughnut and a strawberry thickshake before emerging from my frantic grief would be anything like possible.

For the next ten hours I was swiping for my life, downloading new dating apps I had never even heard of before. As I was scouring through my matches from six months ago that I had never responded to I fell to a new low of whining. 'I'm sick of this. I cannot do it.'

'It was your fucking idea,' the crowd chanted. (The crowd being my housemates who were absolutely right and extremely annoying about it.)

'It's just that, I guess I wanted to be *really* excited about my date – you know? I didn't want it to be just whoever was available. I wanted some flirting and fun and enthusiasm. I wanted to be passionate about this being a compatible person.'

'Post. About. It.' The crowd started harmonising; *Hannah Montana: The Movie* was playing in the background. God, they just loved me (read: were extremely frustrated with my delaying this after forcing them into it).

On the Wednesday morning, forty-eight hours out from the

date, I was attending a launch event for a butt plug. Yes, you read that right. 'The most democratic of all the holes,' I was told at this party. I was excited. I had dressed up more to chat to people and network at the release experience of a vibrating anal toy than I generally did for a first date. Unfortunately, the butt plug would be the one sitting beside and later inside me if I didn't use this fresh face of makeup and hundred-dollar dress to find myself a suitably feminist match. So I walked outside, sat in my car and filmed myself declaring my date-less status. Looking directly into the camera, I confessed my sins.

'Good afternoon all, this is your captain speaking. I have an announcement to make. I am the one who needs a date for this Friday. I was too ashamed to admit it before, but I need your help. I need one of you to step forward or tell me you know the person who should. We have less than forty-eight hours to secure a tall feminist man for the project manager of the group date.'

Beautiful and ashamed, I clicked my heeled boots all the way back into that anal event. I put my phone on aeroplane mode (a classic move for anyone experiencing anxiety after sending or posting something risky) and told everyone at the launch what I was up to. I have quite literally never been mysterious, ever, so I began circling the crowd for takes and opinions. I ate enough cheese and dip at the butt-plug invitational to fill a standard wheelbarrow. This was no different from my usual performance at influencer events, which are attended with my personal motto 'get every freebie, take a hot photo and eat enough that your body is convinced you've just been to a Sizzler buffet'. In a cost-of-living crisis, I was piledriving brie and breadsticks into my mouth as if I were about to hibernate for the winter. Generally I take an extra two bags of PR products and goods for my friends to ensure that in our home there are always three new vibrators, cleansers or vodkas being tried at all times.

I returned to my car two hours later, turned off aeroplane mode and started scrolling through the responses.

Seventeen women had admitted that they thought or secretly wished this was an opportunity to 'turn me' and that they would happily accompany me to the date. It confirmed my longstanding belief that I would slay at being pansexual. I was stoked, but this remained unhelpful, not being my reality on a sweaty January afternoon locked in my car praying to a tiny screen for a miracle. Two men from Darwin offered to fly in for the date. That felt invasive, but good to know I had suitors in a tourist area I was keen to explore in future. A man from Western Australia and one from Melbourne did the same thing. Yikes. This was not landing as swiftly as I had expected. I needed a postcode that started with a two at the very least.

The situation was growing more dire by the minute.

After the event I drove to the only place I knew could support me in these trying times: IKEA. I sat in my heeled black boots, strapless dress and perfectly applied $8 blush and highlighter and ordered a plate of twelve meatballs. I needed mashed potato and lingonberry jam and to feel sorry for myself after my entrée of two wheels of camembert and seventeen pieces of cured meat only an hour before. I wandered through the rooms and picked up a $4 candle, a squid plush toy and a heap of self-esteem after spending a good hour critiquing the showrooms from every angle and deciding I was a better interior decorator than most of the staff at this Swedish icon. As I got to the checkout, a message popped up on Instagram.

'I'll do it, I'm in New South Wales.'

I liked this message. It was not weird or over the top, it was an offer. I looked at this man's profile picture. It was a car. On the page it sounds disgusting, but I'm not talking about a red Commodore with flame stickers. It was a Land Rover Defender pictured in front of a red rocky landscape. I knew this profile. I had seen it before. Clicking on his account, I started browsing through the pictures. I remembered him. Months ago, when I was in a pit of misery about dating apps and the kind of men I was encountering on them, I thought: are all the men who follow Cheek Media, and me, just the partners of feminist women? Or are there actually legit prospects who follow out of their own interest and passion for progressive news commentary? At what I would describe as a low point, I'd clicked on a pretty picture of me on Instagram and started scrolling through the likes in search of this data point. The first man who had liked the image from eight months ago was him. I clicked on his profile and scrolled through the typical hallmark Australian man Instagram. Images of his friends on the beach, beer in hand, and car photo after car photo. He looked kind. He looked tall. I recall thinking 'hot', and with this newfound confidence I exited his profile and went back to my TikTok feed. I had been validated that single, heterosexual-appearing Australian men followed me. I didn't realise I had just stalked my future boyfriend and not done a thing about it.

Minutes after I had replied to his message confirming he was my date for fewer than forty hours later, I received a message from another woman. She was sending me his Instagram profile.

'HANNAH, I promise you, Coen is your man. Six foot four, loves to naked garden and go on adventures, is based in Mid North Coast NSW BUT HE WILL TRAVEL FOR YOU QUEEN.'

A woman's endorsement sealed the deal. I started messaging him consistently until the date. I gave him my phone number and once we were texting he told me that when I initially replied to his date offer he felt like he was having a heart attack at the gym.

'I have had a crush on you for years.'

This feeling was strange. I was at once alarmed that he might have me placed on a pedestal, as many Cheek followers wrongly do, and would inevitably be bitterly disappointed by who I actually am – that the online projection didn't come with my fears, shames, insecurities and baggage, that this was still just a 'more honest' but performed social-media self. I also felt lovely, knowing there were people who found me attractive and that a tall white heterosexual man could be so drawn in by someone who had received many death threats and hateful remarks from men of the same demographic. He knew what he was engaging with, and he was attracted to me because of it – not despite it like so many men I had dated before him, and around whom I'd felt nervous to be truly political, truly opinionated.

I knew he was driving a few hours to get to our house for the date, but I didn't offer him our blow-up mattress. As my housemates said, he's an adult and he can figure it out. We do not need to accommodate, and you do not need to put yourself in an uncomfortable position before you've met him. See what he does. He arrived at the date first, clean and fresh after travelling more than 300 kilometres down the highway in a car with no air conditioning on a forty-degree summer day. He had booked a hotel room and turned up with a loaf of bread he had baked in his breadmaker; under his arm were three plants – one for each of us gals. As soon as he walked through the door I was done. With his back turned as he placed the items on the kitchen bench, Annie, Lilli and I made eyes at each other. We all knew. I was smiling ear to ear.

By the time he left the next day, I was in an unusual state of calm. The date had been fantastic, and for twenty-four hours I was convinced this was the kind of person I wanted to be in a relationship with. I was excited to learn more. Then, I shifted. I drove south to the small beach town of Gerroa to have a night away with two friends. As we swam in the ocean, drank white wine and ordered dinner from the $5 Dominos range, it was a different voice that sang in my head. The anxiety of desperately wanting the men I dated to like me had evaporated, and what arrived in its place was a desperate urge to abandon the ship.

The following week Coen and I planned a weekend away. He would text me that he was thinking about me, that he couldn't stop smiling and that he was excited to see me again. I thought there must be something wrong with him. I became avoidant. I was so turned off by his effort, by his active liking of me and his clear communication regarding it that I felt emotionally overwhelmed. I remember for those first two weeks consistently believing there had to be something wrong with him for enthusiastically trying to date me. This was my conditioning. After two years spent feeling desperate for texts back, plans in advance and compliments, I now felt like I was being smothered. *You are not supposed to like me this much*, I thought. *I'm going to disappoint you and you are going to leave me. This is fake*, my internal voices screamed. *He likes you, and you are not going to live up to the idea he has of you – run.*

Healthy relationships are hard in a different way. My previous experiences were so negative, so anxiety-inducing, that when I felt calm and safe with someone, I convinced myself it was a trick designed to hurt me more than any of the men who had wounded me overtly. At least they were honest in their fuckboy qualities. When I dated people who treated me poorly, I allowed myself the freedom of feeling unworthy of love, and fixated on *their* issues, *their* trauma, agonising with my friends over their poor treatment of me. I used to take their texts to dinner with friends and we'd unpack the mixed messages, flaky responses and Instagram story replies as if we were deciphering a code from the crime scene of a cold case.

These men just did not want a relationship, and definitely didn't want one with me. I would do anything to convince myself otherwise and allow them back into my life whenever they wanted. I now understand that I fed off the pain they caused me. I was the victim, and the way I regained control through that process was by saying that if I were thinner or prettier they would change their mind about me. This wound was an injury I reopened and poured salt into every time they returned, texting out of the blue as if they had not ghosted me six weeks before.

Everything was going exceptionally well in my life, except dating. It became my fixation. I couldn't allow myself to feel joy until I'd convinced someone I deserved their love. My emotional intelligence and my desire to be chosen by one person who didn't see me as everyone else did drove me away from myself. As my psychologist pointed out, deciding I wasn't thin or pretty enough as a justification for their behaviour was an easy narrative bridge for me to regain control. If I starved myself, they'd text me back. It wasn't that they were emotionally unavailable and didn't care: it was because I'm not pretty. I thought I'd be far past these intrusive thoughts, but they engulfed me.

Now, a man who was doing all the things I didn't know were possible made me uncomfortable. I didn't know how to respond to someone who was forthcoming, secure and confident in his feelings. When he offered affection I couldn't handle, when he cooked dinners and booked hotels and carried the mental load because he wanted to, I was suddenly confronted with my own toxic behaviours.

I am in love with someone who drives four hours after work to see me speak at an event, before getting up at 3am to make it back for work the next day. A man who tells me my communication isn't good enough, that I need to work on this avoidance and allow him to show me love. Who sets clear expectations and boundaries and asks for feedback. Who listens attentively to criticism and at the end of me pouring my soul out for an hour about every fear and concern and worry does not shut down, but asks if there's anything else he can do or work on. Who brings the dinner ingredients and makes the drinks and has a much better skincare routine and is cleaner and more organised than me. Someone who notices even the slightest bodily cue or change during sex and stops to ask if everything is okay. Someone who calls when he says he will and challenges my fear of affection and asks me to explain my anxiety and show him objective evidence for the thought spirals I'm having about myself and the relationship. Someone who asked me if I wanted children and how many on our third date, because he saw long-term potential in our relationship. He just wanted me to know that he liked me. He then wanted me to know that he loved me.

One of the most common responses from women when they learned about my relationship was to say things like, 'Girl, you won.' Because being loved truly, honestly and continuously by a man in a way that is secure, consistent and healthy is a competition with very few prizes in a patriarchal world. To be seen and loved by a man who is not only comfortable with strong, independent, feminist women, but only wants to help nurture that comfortably without taking the spotlight, space or control, is rare. He is not submissive; he is challenging. He is considered, he listens to me, he gives me feedback and takes on mine. He actively works on himself, and is emotionally attuned to his insecurities and flaws. That is considered an Olympic gold medal for men, but the bare minimum for women. The 'jackpot' in a heterosexual relationship is what I would describe as the baseline of all of my female friends, but our platonic love is considered fundamentally subordinate to romantic bonds. It may be controversial, but when the standards for men are so low in our current dating landscape and wider society, specifically when it comes to sex, pleasure and emotional closeness, can women ever truly explore or know their sexuality?

In her fiction bestseller *Good Material*, Dolly Alderton wrote:

> I once heard a theory about the first relationship that occurs after a big relationship ends. It is called the 90/10 rule. The theory goes: whatever the crucial 10 per cent is that was missing from your partner who was otherwise totally right for you is the thing you look for in the following person. That missing 10 per cent becomes such a fixation that, when you do find someone who has it, you ignore the fact they do not have the other 90 per cent that the previous partner had.

I found this to be true of my entire dating experience. Every one of my long-term relationships had been loving and supportive, but in the aftermaths of these breakups I became fixated on men who had the things I believed I wanted in a partner. These 'things' (I describe them as 'things' not 'qualities' because they were achievements, not values) came at the expense of kindness, respect, emotional and mental labour and effort that my boyfriends had provided me in previous partnerships. These horrendous dating experiences taught me much about myself and what I thought I wanted, in contrast to what I actually valued in someone I wanted to spend a longer, more committed part of my life with. I wonder how my life would be different if I did end up committed – even for a couple of years – to one of the men I dated who was not emotionally present. I believe it would have eroded a central part of me that would have taken a long time to rebuild. I may never have healed. I may have suffered in the same way my mother did and in the way I have watched so many of my friends do.

My best friends have asked me if it's too soon to be writing these stories, to be committing to paper a new relationship and sexual experiences I haven't yet wholly processed. But I believe this is exactly why it's important I get it all down now, learning and reflecting as it happens. I have never wanted nor expected that the words I write will withstand years of maturing and changing. They can't. If they do, that means neither the world nor I have progressed at the rate I hope we do. I can't control the future; I can't control my relationships or other people's experiences. Part of that is writing how I feel without attempting to take hold of the outcome.

I am in love now, and it is the most glorious thing I have ever experienced. If that changes, I will still be brilliant. That's what I want all women to know. You will continue as an exceptional, loved person. The goal is not to be partnered; the goal is to know and love yourself enough to continue being vulnerable and bold with your life. I know I can and I will. The difference now is I have a blueprint for the kind of relationship I want: the one I have right now.

4
Work

taboo 6:

✖

Motherhood Is Work; 'Having it All' Is Dead

Women are not going to be equal outside the home
until men are equal in it.

Gloria Steinem

It was a rainy afternoon in the middle of an Orange winter. I was in year eleven, and to describe myself kindly, I was a heinous bitch who would start an argument with my mother for saying she liked my top. I didn't want to know my parents. I wanted to eat their food and live under their roof and tell them I was smarter than them every day instead. I was a delight to be around on fewer than 1.5 days per month. Mum was having coffee with a friend, and they were dropping me at work on their way to the main street. I was the intruder on their friendship, scrolling in the backseat, probably scanning My Fitness Pal or another calorie counting app that told me I was obese for consuming more than a celery stick. I was miserable and revolting, on my way to stack shelves until 9pm for $15 an hour.

'If I had my time over again, I wouldn't have children,' Mum said rather jovially in the front seat.

I had been blurred out of their conversation, instead busily applying a filter to my Snapchat for mass send-out. Suddenly, the pierce of her words brought the world into sharp focus. I chose to hear: 'I do not want you here. I regret your existence. I would take it all away. I do not want to be your mum. You are ruining my life.' These are all the distortions that twisted through my brain. I heard my mum, but I did not listen to her.

Like any teenager can be expected to do, I made it an attack on me as a person. I saw it only as a reflection that I was not enough for my mum. Motherhood had not lived up to her expectations.

The sting of these words lasted years, seared into my memory. It festered, an open wound I would pour salt into every now and then when we would fight. Only now, ruminating on my own decision-making and thoughts about children and family, do I ever really consider the person my mum is, the mother she has been, and what she might have been like before I met her.

Within months of this conversation eight years ago, my mum told my dad their marriage was over. He proceeded to stalk her, become violent and speak poorly of her to everyone in our small town who'd listen. He then moved interstate, stranding her in single parenthood. As my name was written down on the emergency contact for my siblings on every school form, extracurricular activity and lesson, I resented them both. I put my head down and refused to talk to my teachers or attend psychologist appointments. I finished my HSC and got a scholarship to study law in Queensland.

In the years following, Mum raised my brother and sister alone in regional New South Wales. She was self-employed, running multiple businesses, and working full-time as a public servant, still helping me where she could. Meanwhile, my dad would ring me to complain that his tax return was not good because the government took out all the child support he had not been paying.

I look at Mum differently now. I see a girl I had never cared to meet before. I wonder what she gossiped about at the back of the school bus with her friends. I want to see her pack the outfits she had decided on for an overseas trip. I think about her sitting cross-legged on the floor in front of a mirror getting ready for a night out with seven rejected tops strewn across the bedroom floor. The woman I knew was someone who had not wanted children, but loved a charismatic man who proposed a life that was incredibly fun, until it wasn't.

What my mum said as a throwaway comment in the car was sharp, because it went against the grain. She said something women are not allowed to say. I couldn't understand a view that had never been presented to me before, that women were able to envision a different path for themselves. My friends' mums would never say what my mum did, and I took offence where I now see bravery. She didn't say she regretted me: she said that she wanted her choice to have been more free than it was. Existing in a present that is working hard to normalise being childfree by choice highlights the utter absence of that option (especially for women) twenty-five years ago.

My mum didn't choose to have three babies over seven years, with miscarriages in between. She didn't choose to work full-time in a role that paid her $40,000 less than my father in the same company. I'm sure it was not her dream to cook every meal, do every load of washing and always drive my dad home from his big nights out with a smile on her face. I do not think she anticipated begging him for love for more than a decade, only to be met with the silent treatment. Mum did not mean she does not want to be my mum: she meant she did and does not want a motherhood of exclusion from society. She does not want a motherhood of barriers. She does not want a motherhood of isolation and abuse and exhaustion. When my mum told her friend she wouldn't have children if she had her time over again, she meant she wanted to be Philippa for longer – not Mum. If our society had been able to see her as Philippa, not my mum, the decision to step into the role of mother might have been a lot more enticing.

My mum wants to be seen as a person first, by her partner and her children. My mum wants to have the same super-annuation balance as my dad and to come home to a clean house and kick up her feet and wonder when dinner is and complain about it being stroganoff, just like we did. When I undervalue my mum, when I see her only as an extension of myself and not as an individual person, I participate in the undermining of motherhood. If I had not come to this awareness, it wouldn't be until I fell into the very same trap that I realised. Now I know I do not really want to be a mother, but being a father sounds fucking fantastic. Now, I want to ask my mum every question under the sun to find every fault in the system.

It was only when I contemplated my own thoughts around becoming a mother that it became so clear. I didn't ever see motherhood as my purpose, but as one of the things I wanted to be. Why had I not afforded the same personhood to the woman who made, carried, birthed and raised me? Society failed our mums. I failed my mum by failing to understand what she was required to do in order for me to sit here and write this today. Despite constantly remarking that she wants grandchildren, in that moment, when I was still in high school, my mum gave me permission to choose. From the age of seventeen, I knew that she supported me as a woman just as I am, not primarily as a mother. In a society that still does not want women to have that choice, it was opened to me by the woman who carried me.

So, as I write a chapter on work, I'm not going to agonise over climbing the man-made corporate ladder. Being overworked and burned out is glorified, not taboo. The taboo is what sits beneath the LinkedIn post that managed to use the terms *journey, empowered* and *investment banking* in the same sentence without flinching at the moral bankruptcy of it all.

Motherhood is work. Work is unpaid domestic labour. It is caring responsibilities; the mental load. Women do not work less than men: the issue is that neither men nor women value women's work. Our economy does not account for it, and unpaid work isn't recognised in official economic statistics. According to the Committee for Economic Development of Australia, the value of the unpaid work undertaken by Australians each year totals around $570 billion, with two-thirds of this contributed by women. According to Oxfam estimates, if women received minimum wage for all the unpaid care and domestic labour they perform, this would contribute almost $11 trillion to the global economy annually. That's around 9 per cent of global gross domestic product. This number, read in Oxfam's reporting, is more than three times the size of the global tech industry.

The default question for women who question becoming mothers is: why don't you want to have children?

But it should be: why *would* I want to have children?

Why would I want to bring a child into a world that does not value mothers?

Why would I want to bring a child into a world that does not value the future that child will inherit?

Why would I bring a child into a world I cannot afford to live in, let alone support my baby in?

Why would I risk my health and safety in a world that does not believe my reproductive choices are my own to make?

Why would I give birth in an environment rife with barriers that exclude me from communities I once thrived in?

The reason I want to become a mother is because I want to love and care for my child. I want to help someone grow. I want to teach them and guide them and mentor them into adulthood. But if I cannot love and care for myself, if the society I live in cannot help me do those things, I can't do it for another person.

The women who believe what I'm saying is absurd either have the privilege of wealth and assistance, or they are willing to look past the unnecessary, society-imposed suffering required in the pursuit of motherhood. They might say they'd do it again in a heartbeat – I'm sure I would, too. But does our ability as mothers to survive in these conditions actually act as encouragement? Why are we surprised women are terrified of the prospect of being unsupported in their transition to the most important role of all?

Women spend 64.4 per cent of their average weekly working time on unpaid care work compared to 36.1 per cent for men. This is a 'gender time gap in unpaid care work' according to the Workplace Gender Equality Agency. Mothers are valued in spirit, in essence, in language alone. This valuation does not bleed into the practical experience of what it is to mother, to raise the next generation. What patriarchy requires is the elevation of the status of 'the mother' as a means of retaining power over women. They do not value mothers: they value control of our bodies. Australia's Time Use Survey reported that women are being paid for 45 per cent of their contribution to the economy, in contrast to men's 69 per cent. The research found that Australian women undertake $771 worth of unpaid work each week, compared to men's unpaid work amounting to less than $500. As Dr Leonora Risse wrote for *The Sydney Morning Herald* on this evidence, 'in real terms, that equates to a domestic labour pay gap of over 50 per cent. [It] makes the workplace gender pay gap look positively mild in comparison.'

The gap must be explained, because most people have no idea what it means. The gender pay gap, as defined by the Australian Government's Workplace Gender Equality Agency, reflects the difference between the average earnings of women and men in the workforce. It is the result of social and economic factors that reduce women's earning capacity over the course of their lifetimes. It is important to distinguish this from the difference between two people being paid differently for work of the same or comparable value, which is 'unequal pay'. This is unlawful.

The gender pay gap stems from systemic cultural issues within capitalism. It mirrors the historic misconceptions and undervaluing of women's contributions to the workforce, the lack of workplace flexibility to accommodate caring responsibilities in a society where women take on a greater share of the domestic and unpaid labour, the underrepresentation of women in leadership and management positions, and the historic discrepancy between the wages and value placed on male-dominated versus female-dominated industries.

Conscious and unconscious bias plays a significant role in hiring, remuneration and promotions. This is not limited to gender. This discrimination is only exacerbated when we consider other factors including race, disability, age and sexuality. It is vital that we understand and reflect on how these overlapping aspects of a person's identity expose them to amplified and compounded forms of discrimination. Women's earnings fall by 55 per cent in the first five years of parenthood, while men's earnings remain unaffected, a Treasury analysis found in 2022. The penalty persists for at least a decade into parenthood. This only scratches the surface of the impacts of career interruptions, unpaid labour and caring responsibilities.

We must challenge the narrative that women invariably *choose* to work part-time or stay home and care for their families. We know that the cost of childcare and the stereotypical cultural expectations surrounding care and parenting roles means that women are presented with little choice but to step back from full-time work. The superannuation gap sees women retire with a third less superannuation than men do, according to the Super Members Council. The superannuation gap between men and women in some age groups is as high as 47.8 per cent.

The gender pay gap is rejected as an issue most often by those who are not only not impacted by it, but who benefit from it. Men tell themselves and others that the gap is due to choices women make, not a system that has forced them out of paid work and imposed the belief that their contributions lack economic value. The biggest myths around the gender pay gap and the central points of arguments against its existence often surround individual pay comparisons within specific workplaces and the view that women elect to stop working or aren't capable of the hours men work. These arguments lack nuance, ignore social norms and cultural expectations and pass over how a causal chain of events continues to enforce a gender hierarchy. It is not about how many hours are put in, the quality of the work, our 'natural qualities' or industries women 'gravitate towards'. This is a socially constructed and conditioned belief system. It is factually incorrect.

A KPMG study run over fifty years found that when the presence of women increases in a particular industry, the pay rate declines. Every industry in Australia has a gender pay gap that favours men, according to the Workplace Gender Equality Agency. Women's work is seen as inferior. When we partner the expectation that women are meant to be in the home with a lack of workplace flexibility, we find another culminating factor that reduces our perceived viability for senior leadership and management positions. Men move upwards because of the women they rely on staying down to manage households and families – and having a family elevates their workplace and public reputation.

In her fiction work *Motherhood*, Sheila Heti subverts the commonly held belief that a woman is a through line to the next generation, not an independent being:

It seemed to me like all my worrying about not being a mother came down to this history – this implication that a woman is not an end in herself. She is a means to a man, who will grow up to be an end in himself, and do something in the world. While a woman is a passageway through which a man might come. I have always felt like an end in myself – does not everyone? – but perhaps my doubt that being an end-in-myself is enough comes from this deep lineage of women not being seen as ends, but as passageways through which a man might come. If you refuse to be a passageway, there is something wrong. You must at least *try*. But

I do not want to be a passageway through which a man might come, then manifest himself in the world however he likes, without anyone doubting his right.

One of my constant battles is the feeling that, if women do not become mothers, they are expected to do something earth-shattering instead. There must be a business, a creative endeavour or extensive travel. If not motherhood, there must be something that occupies her every waking thought. What if we wanted the ability to choose to have our own time, our own space, our own independent lives free from caring? We know the data. Women with higher education have fewer children: this is because educated people have more opportunities for productive lives doing work other than childrearing. Globally, research shows that as education levels rise, fertility levels fall. But even the use of the word 'productive' strips us of our abilities to escape the capitalist machine. What if women don't want to work all the time? What if we want to just live outside our titles?

Women can be the biggest critics of women who choose to be childfree. In my experience, the strongest bias applied to a woman who does not want children is the belief that she is criticising those who do. That one decision is evidence of a hatred for or a resentment of all children and all people who parent. Why is an individual's choice a judgement of or a statement about another? Not wanting children does not mean one lacks maternal urges or is a hater of children. Why is the avoidance of this one act so tightly bound to the identity of childfree women? Why is something we *are* not more important and inherent to our identity, than what we choose not to be? This is an argument of division, one where we are unable to progress so long as we are at war with each other and ignoring the root of the problem. It is a particular kind of loneliness to not long for the things most others seem to. To walk an entirely different path is rewarding but isolating. I believe I want to have children. Yet if I do not have children, I know I will have more time, more opportunity to explore myself and the world, and more freedom to choose. Society is offended by those who walk a different path. I wonder how often that is because they feel they cannot express their own regret. I love and want children, but I want to be selfish with my life, too.

Women have been sold a lie that we are born to mother, to clean, to organise, to maintain homes. There has been a careful and strategic categorisation by patriarchy of particular traits as being either masculine or feminine. Not only is this untrue, but it teaches women that it is in our nature to be more empathetic, to take on caring roles, and that we are intensely more emotional than men. The flow-on effect of this is men having permission to lack emotional intelligence, *and* it teaches women who do not want to do the unpaid work of caregiving and emotional labour that they are somehow lesser women. If society continues to impose the view that we have no control over these characteristics, and that they are inherent from birth, it reinforces the gender divide and narrows the scope of what we as humans can be. Katie Jgln writes:

> Insisting that women are more 'delicate' or are naturally more predisposed to be 'kind and caring' can seem harmless or even positive, but it is actually a form of sexism, too – benevolent sexism ... And while hostile sexism might be easier to spot, it is the benevolent sexism that's far more insidious. After all, it perpetuates reductive gender stereotypes that ultimately justify women's subordinate position in society, all under the pretence that it is 'for our own good.'

This sentiment is extended in Gina Rushton's book *The Most Important Job in the World*, as she explores the cognitive dissonance between the way the ruling class claims to uphold motherhood while politically degrading women's rights. She writes about reporting on parliamentary debates in which 'physical sovereignty was debated by men who fetishised motherhood, the most important job in the world, while supporting policies that made life harder for mothers.' Government policies, media, financial institutions and large corporations convey the need to 'increase women's labour force participation', but that language is repeatedly failing to reflect women's experience of labour. Mothers are contributing to the workforce; this work is just not seen or defined as such. This intersects and compounds with both race and class issues. Women who must work to provide for their children are either deemed 'bad mothers' or even criminalised for leaving their children in order to earn a wage to feed them. The experience of poverty or not being white means the lens applied to your work is not that of a 'girl boss' but of a failure. Society not only fails but actively oppresses these women, and then punishes them for any subsequent choice they make in the pursuit of survival.

Women's domestic work ensures that men are able to participate in the paid workforce at higher rates, and are then considered harder working, more successful and more capable than women. The reality is it isn't women's productivity or participation that needs to be transformed or uplifted: it is men's. Men need to do more unpaid labour in order for that labour to be considered valuable to society. Women's wider participation depends on men's capacity to support us by doing the work our culture deems to be 'caretaking' and therefore inferior. Bri Lee made the comparison perfectly in an interview with Camilla + Marc: 'We're not going to get the ideal future for women until we have mandatory, use-it-or-lose-it paid parental leave for all genders. Until we make employers as terrified that a man will become a father as they currently are of women becoming mothers, you will never stop discrimination in the workplace.'

This is one of the most straightforward, practical solutions possible to the problem of inequality in the workforce and of the need for unpaid labour. We need a cultural shift, led by policy, that forces men into primary caregiving roles. Men need to be expected to be parents to the extent that women are. The gender pay gap is not a 'choice' women are making: it is an expectation imposed on women since the moment we are handed a Baby Born at the age of two. Care is learned, and it's expected that joy and fulfilment will come from performing it.

Our capitalist society relies on free labour. It relies on cheap labour. It relies on those performing this labour to be told they are being demanding, and causing inflation, when they ask for that labour to be paid fairly and to accompany a set of working rights that protects their humanity. It relies on a tiered valuation of labour that ensures the bulk of hard, domestic work is separated from productivity and from economic valuation. It relies on women and minorities quietly trying to stay afloat, believing they deserve no more.

I've often seen rhetoric proposing that being a stay-at-home parent is somehow antifeminist, the central argument being that these individuals lack financial independence, and can become vulnerable in circumstances of violence, abuse and the decrease in stability and career prospects they experience after time away from the workforce. The issue is in the concealment of privilege. When it comes to wealth, resources and help, the issue is always the innate belief of those with privilege that it is possible for anyone to do what they do. In a piece for *The Guardian*, columnist Rhiannon Lucy Cosslett articulates this distinction:

> Stay-at-home mums are often left out of these discussions because their existence is inconvenient to both sides. Women who actively want to be stay-at-home mums are uncomfortable for some feminists to contemplate because they have traditionally been so lionise. And the stay-at-home mum is threatening to the other side of the debate because capitalism relies on free domestic labour. She can be encouraged and deified as long as she doesn't consider what she is doing as work worthy of financial recompense. The minute she does that, she becomes dangerous.

The focus for feminism should not be on getting stay-at-home mothers to enter the workforce they prop up. It should be on paying them for their contributions and getting men to take on the role in turn. In *The Most Important Job in the World*, Gina Rushton also examines this with acute skill:

> You only have to look at the wages of childcare workers, teachers and aged care workers to see how this lingering presumption complements a 'do what you love' ethos to

devalue work that is traditionally gendered female. Care work in the home has been denigrated for so long that it still fails to be compensated fairly outside of it. Looking back, I see clearly how equating my paid labour with my own value in society was not just foolish but in direct opposition with how I value other people. It does not square with how I value the time and effort of my brother, an unemployed person living in social housing, nor how I value my mother's domestic care on the days she was not teaching. Any progress, particularly for women, that confines itself to the workplace feels to me now not just incomplete but exclusionary. In overvaluing paid employment, we devalue what is underpaid or unpaid and allow the state to continue shafting the burdens of social reproduction on to families.

While the girl-boss corner of the feminist movement has often shamed women for opting to stay at home, the point has been missed entirely. What if instead of shaming a woman for wanting to be at home, society valued and paid for her work? What would the outcomes be for children, women and men if caring responsibilities and domestic labour were paid work? Women who wish they could stay at home are not necessarily wanting to be tradwives, who act as subservient slaves, believing they are inferior to men. Tradwives are extremist opponents of feminism – fuelled by religion and conservatism – and they are the minority. Most women performing the impossible juggle of 'having it all' are just fighting to raise children above the poverty line. They want to contribute, retain their identities but also have a family of this nature. Not wanting 'it all' is not antifeminist; in fact, the pursuit of a well-balanced, joyful life without judgement is at the centre of what feminism fights for. In her 1974 book on the social consequences of domestic labour, *Wages Against Housework*, Silvia Federici wrote:

The difference lies in the fact that not only has housework been imposed on women, but it has been transformed into a natural attribute of our female physique and personality, an internal need, an aspiration, supposedly coming from the depth of our female character. Housework had to be transformed into a natural attribute rather than be recognized as a social contract because from the beginning of capital's scheme for women this work was destined to be unwaged. Capital had to convince us that it is a natural, unavoidable and even fulfilling activity to make us accept our unwaged work. In its turn, the unwaged condition of housework has been the most powerful weapon in reinforcing the common assumption that housework is not work, thus preventing women from struggling against it, except in the privatized kitchen–bedroom quarrel that all society agrees to ridicule, thereby further reducing the protagonist of a struggle. We are seen as nagging bitches, not workers in struggle.

Wanting to be a mother and not wanting to work yourself to death in the process is not antifeminist. It's antipatriarchy and anticapitalist. We need to stop shaming each other and start dismantling a system that expects us to work for our own families. Men outsourcing work is considered efficient – time saved that frees up their capacity to provide. Women are shamed for their inability to cook and clean – how many times have you heard a woman exclaim that she must 'clean before the cleaner' or that it would be far too expensive and embarrassing to pay for help at all? Women's desire to earn money and to be supported is a stain on our femininity, but men's outsourcing of household duties is strategic and effective – it's just business, really. I often think about this. Two of my close friends, Annabel Phelan and Rory McGahan, founded a business, Dara, to reduce women's invisible labour. The first time I met them, I learned more about the mental load and the research behind gendered labour than I would have in an entire university course. One of the most significant points they made is how the outsourcing of work considered 'men's labour' is more acceptable than that of socially perceived 'women's work'. To get your car professionally washed, have your yard maintained by a gardener or have a tradie fix a pipe, a fridge or your toilet is far more acceptable than it is for women to hire cleaners or carers or to outsource home management. Men's 'jobs' are also occasional and finite; they have a clear and defined ending. Mowing the lawn is more visible and defined than the endlessness of washing, feeding and tidying. Fundamentally, spending money on work that women are expected to do for free is positioned as more shameful than the professionalised industries of male-dominated work.

The gender pay gap enables the gender shame gap. Women stay home to manage the home because it seems ludicrous to pay for services that would empower a woman to re-enter the workforce. The cost of childcare is considered too much for women to return to a job that doesn't see their value anyway. These calculations are generally made against the salary of the mother, not proportionally from the couple as a unit in circumstances in which both parents are present. Childcare is a mother's deduction, not a benefit that serves both parents equally. As women fight to earn more while continuing to manage the labour of our homes, we must ask ourselves less about how to keep women in work and instead how to get men to value women's work, primarily by getting them into the home. The valuation of women's work going up depends on men being expected to do it.

When Annabel Crabb wrote *The Wife Drought* in 2014, she published the bible on the work–life balance that has failed modern women and, if anything, regressed:

Have a look at the results when Australians are asked if they agree or disagree with the statement: 'It is better for the family if the husband is the principal breadwinner outside the home and the wife has primary responsibility for the home and children.' In 1986, just over 55 per cent of men agreed with that proposition. That proportion swan-dived down to about 30 per cent by 2001, but by 2005, it had gone up again, to 41.4 per cent. Women subscribe to that view less enthusiastically than men on the whole, but they too have waxed and waned over the last thirty years. In 1986, 33 per cent of them thought it was better for men to work and women to keep house. By 2001, that had dipped to 19 per cent. But by 2005, it had bobbed back up to 36.4 per cent.

When we say women are striving to 'have it all', we mean all of the labour. We aren't going to move the needle by continuing to suffer in silence while putting on a brave face. The answer is to relinquish the shame we have been feeling for 'failing' in our roles and responsibilities in the home, and the need to perform to the girl-boss standards of millennial feminism.

The true solution is this: men need to do 'women's work'. Women need to dismantle the shame of outsourcing the work we have been conditioned to believe is ours by right. If your partner believes it is embarrassing to be a primary carer, what does that say about his view of women? Of you? Truly. It is time that we understand the value of our contributions to society and rewrite the narrative. Our work is valuable, whatever that work looks like. We should be paid, we should be seen and we should be supported on whatever path we take. The first step to asserting that worth is by believing it ourselves. The next is to ask, as Crabb does, 'Why, after all these decades of campaign, reform, research and thought about how we can best get women into the workplace, are we so slow to pick up that the most important next step is how to get men out of it?'

ten rules for life: women and money edition

1. Women: do not ask for more money, do not flaunt money and do not even think about flexible work arrangements or a liveable wage.

2. Also, please do not have money. Be very very Quiet Luxury about it.

3. If you own property, you are a capitalist. If you don't own property, work harder and stop getting your nails done or feeling joy until you do.

4. Finance and economics are not your space: please go back to the industries we have designated to you, and that we also decided are worth less or nothing while you were very busy not looking at us building this system that exploits you.

5. Every time you go on a date a man will explain to you why we can't print more money. This is heterosexual law.

6. Your superannuation will be far less than men's, even though you work far more across your lifetime.

7. Please be thankful that you are now allowed to work and have a credit card in your own name. This is a privilege, and one that your grandmother didn't have.

8. Rich men are aspirational businessmen; rich women should be ashamed for hoarding all that money.

9. His PlayStation is a good spend; your interior decor trinkets are frivolous and unacceptable.

10. Have a copy of *The Barefoot Investor* on your coffee table.

taboo 7:

✖

Money Money Money

'Show me your bank account.'

It's a statement that sits on my lips every day. I whisper it into my phone late at night, and with every swipe of my thumb, every drag up the screen of my phone, it becomes louder.

Another European summer. A *SOLD* sign on another home. Wedding. Cosmetic surgery. Baby shower. Engagement party. Another designer dress. Renovations. Diamond ring. Cutting that new-car ribbon with comical scissors. Just a spontaneous six months overseas. How much for that #PaidPartnership. Summer boat party. LinkedIn promotion with a wanky self-serving paragraph. I googled her top from that post: $400 second-hand. They are on another international trip and it's only April. Have I ever seen them wear an outfit twice? Do everyone's parents have money except me?

I'm jealous of wealthy people. More than that, actually: I'm resentful, shockingly so. Let me be clear: it's not because I want to wear high-end brands or even pretend to. I don't aspire to fine dining, where you leave a meal starving because you paid $46 a course for a thin slice of wagyu and a drip of sauce the name of which you can't pronounce. I don't wish for the pressures that come with the upper-class culture of upkeep: trends to follow and private schools and job titles and last names and social circles that don't mean a fucking thing. I dream of *ease*. I want to not check my bank balance before I tap my phone on the bill for dinner, and I want to pay for my friends just because. I think about my mum buying a nice pair of shoes for herself without having to hide the shopping bag from my dad as we walked into our home on a Sunday morning. I imagine purchasing a property without needing to 'give up' the joy of the day-to-day for years in the pursuit of an increasingly impossible deposit. I wonder what it would be like to scroll through Instagram and not feel pangs of anger every time I see an outfit, a holiday, an experience, a wedding or a home that I know was paid for with a bank balance or access to credit I have never known the feeling of. Most of all I hate how much I hate it. How much I wonder, how much

I judge, how much I resent, fear, aspire to and feel shame around money. It is my untouched taboo.

My mother was raised in a wealthy family; my father was raised in a poor one. As a child, my home life fluctuated between middle class and lower middle class as my parents moved jobs and cities. In primary school, we lived in a low socioeconomic area of Sydney in a home my parents built and I considered us to be wealthy in the area we resided (we had Foxtel in 2010 and went to Pizza Hut once a month, which to primary-school me was about as rich as you can get). When we moved to Orange during my high school years in 2012, my parents struggled to find work and Mum picked up multiple jobs to keep us afloat. I contributed to the home with part-time work. I paid my own way through university and received multiple scholarships. I will not receive an inheritance, and there is unlikely to be any secret gold mine uncovered in the next decade to propel me into comfort. If my business fails, there isn't a safety net. I loan my parents money, not the other way around.

My relationship with finance has been one of ignorance and fear. Growing up in a household that was never financially stable or consistent left me feeling not only financially illiterate, but also that spending money is a risk. I pride myself on making complex topics accessible, so I buy money books (that sit unread and untouched on my bedside table), follow every women's financial Instagram account and google 'what does ASX stand for' more frequently than I care to admit. I check my balance before I tap my card for a coffee, hide my Amazon order of cheap pimple patches and sometimes buy a $300 dress because it makes me feel happy and I don't want to purchase things made in a sweatshop (despite the Amazon package arriving an hour before). Wealth makes me nervous. I worry I will become wealthy and lose connection with my values. I also worry I will never be wealthy, and I will constantly stress about my income and savings and prospective debt. Is this normal?

I don't resent that someone has a million dollars, but I believe having a billion dollars should be a criminal offence. I know that my hatred for money, at its root, is in the silence. The origin of the taboo around finance is not in the existence of money, but in the lack of transparency with which it is moved, taken, hoarded. This is the origin of all taboos, but it is unparalleled when it comes to wealth. Money is something not only obscured from the world, but within our most intimate relationships. Pay secrecy clauses, which prevented employees from disclosing their salaries (and therefore ensuring that colleagues in the same job were paid at the same rate), were only banned last year in Australia. Some of the most common feminist questions I see debated involve the financial dynamics of romantic relationships and the financial inequality of friendship. From the personal cost for bridesmaids in a wedding party to the inequality in earnings when starting a family with a partner, there are inconclusive debates and discussions that invade our bank accounts and reflect our own relationships with financial literacy and wealth. What we choose to spend money on and why fundamentally alters the power dynamics of our social worlds. As the wealth gap becomes a cavern, the quality of our conversations to combat this decreases. In her *Refinery29* piece, 'If you grew up with money, stop being weird about it', Daisy Jones cracks open the taboo that accompanies wealth:

Being born into money is not some value judgement or a moral failing on your part – it just means you had a bit of a leg up, because society sucks and is built that way. Hearing rich people downplay their richness feels a bit like when skinny people complain about feeling 'fat' after a big lunch – as if it is the same as being unable to access healthcare as a fat person. There's a big difference between the way something makes you feel and how it concretely impacts other people's lives. This idea that money shouldn't be acknowledged or 'visible' is actually built into the way many rich people communicate. For example, you've probably heard the term 'nouveau riche'. It means 'new money' and is used to describe those who haven't inherited wealth but freshly acquired it. It's often thrown at people who are gauche with their richness, buying things that are openly expensive rather than low-key and understated. This is because nothing says 'money' like pretending you do not have money, whether through secrecy or minimalism. Which is weird when you think about it. People spend so much time protecting and acquiring something that must not be spoken about and only ever alluded to, like a subtle wink between friends.

In a capitalist society, your wealth is your worth. As women, that becomes even more nuanced. Earn enough, but not too much. Be quiet in your luxury. It's excessive. Be quiet in your poverty, too. It's embarrassing. Author of *Financial Feminist* and founder of organisation Her First 100k, Tori Dunlap, summarised the gendered nature of building wealth in an interview with Audible:

For men, it is about building wealth. It is not about limiting; it is about expanding. It's about how to increase your salary, how to increase the amount of money coming in, how to invest in real estate and the stock market. And for women, it is deprive yourself. It is not 'go earn more money or go make more money'. It is spend less money on things we deem as 'frivolous' – manicures, a little latte, Dior purses. So that in and of it itself is extremely gendered language: men, build; women, deprive.

But specifically, we are asking women to stop spending money on the very thing that we expect them to do in society, which is perform femininity in a certain way. You're not going to be able to see the video of this, but I'm showing up at this interview without makeup, I haven't done my hair in a while and the roots have grown out. I am not performing femininity in a certain way. So, the very thing we're shaming women for spending money on – manicures, makeup, waxing, fashion – is the very thing that then, if you show up at work without it, you get called tired. Or if I show up at a job interview without makeup, I'm deemed 'unprofessional', and I'm putting this in air quotes. And if you are a woman of color, especially a Black woman, we see this even more predominantly.

Financial messaging tends to be advertised as self-help and self-improvement. In the pursuit of growth, women are taught to improve their own circumstances and experiences of the world. Look wealthy but don't be wealthy. While education around finance is an incredibly powerful tool, we need to understand that it is less about self-help and more about privilege. This is another facet of the self-improvement cycle that encourages women to have enough money to keep up appearances, style and health. Earn so much you can afford to maintain yourself, but do not work so much that we see the strain. It is a dichotomy that creates an attitude of money dysmorphia: a constant confusion of our financial status in an uncertain, unaffordable world. I feel guilt for buying nice things, and also when I buy a cheaper, unsustainable product. I am more likely to buy a $17 burger than a $20 T-shirt. Is it a symptom of a younger generation that I feel this is such a battle? I believe we are about to enter an anticelebrity era, and with that will come a reckoning on the public flaunting of luxury.

The richest 1 per cent of people now own just less than half the world's wealth. In Australia, 2024 reporting by the Australian Council of Social Service and UNSW Sydney found that almost half of all wealth is held by the richest 10 per cent of households: they hold fifteen times the wealth of the lowest 60 per cent. Wealth inequality is the greatest issue of our time, but there is cognitive dissonance in my hatred of seeing influencers flaunt their ability to afford a designer dress, when instead my focus should be on the ultra-rich who hoard resources and power in the same volume as cash. My criticism is gendered; my internalised misogyny is showing. There is a distinction between being able to buy a fancy dress for a party and those who reside within the top 1 per cent – though this hierarchy is becoming more apparent with maintained pressure from generation Z audiences on celebrities to acknowledge their privilege and use it to benefit those who are marginalised.

I believe following the rich and famous as a form of aspiration and entertainment will die as the dystopic juxtaposition of events such as the Met Gala and global warfare continues to destabilise audiences of millions. I think young people's commitment to social causes outweighs our fandom of the artists and entertainers we love – but that might just be my echo chamber. To me, it matters how money is spent and possessed. While I don't agree that social media communities should demand political content from all creators and users, I do see the future of these platforms as being a public square of truer democracy in the space of creation and conversation. I am more likely to follow, be influenced by and engage with a person filming in a home that looks like mine than a model telling me to not worry about the Easter chocolate I eat this Sunday. I am going to be happier with an algorithm full of people giving me realistic advice, sharing honest thoughts and telling stories than with a feed of 'everything I eat in a day' videos from those who can afford a private chef.

We exist in an online chasm where we are choosy in who influences us, and we have an active conscience, so we anticipate that the people we see reflect the values we live. I don't necessarily agree with this approach, that we can demand relatability or commentary from public figures, but it's difficult to deny that this is the way our following list is moving. 'Influence', for generation Z, is only as strong as a creator's ability to consider and take on audience feedback. Creators don't need to listen to all of it, but they must understand the flow of public opinion and responsibilities that come with the role and burden of 'influence'. Social media, especially through the growing presence of personable, more organic platforms like TikTok, is increasingly becoming a space for equal conversations that thrive on relatability. The rich and famous come to die here, because they prove just how out of touch they really are. Influence is now less about what your audience aspires to be, and instead how authentically high-profile individuals are meeting society at their level. As the wealth gap increases, the capacity of celebrities to see and engage with their fans decreases. The future of influence belongs to those who are not tied to their money and are capable of seeing and acting on their privilege for the better.

While much of this remains a taboo or at least controversial subject, the reason I have any understanding of wealth inequality is that people have dedicated their online spaces to breaking down the shame we feel around money. There are content creators on social media, in the podcasting space and operating entire sections of publications dedicated to financial transparency and literacy. It isn't all doom and gloom. Some creators are responding to the cost-of-living crisis by breaking down cheap home-cooked meals while others fight for better protections for renters and educate others on their housing and employment rights. The democratisation of the public square through new forms of media has given everyday people the opportunity to talk about the financial and economic hierarchy and the small, effective ways we can work to combat our own oppression. It has never been our responsibility to fight these powerful institutions, but my fear of money will never lead to my own safety or comfort. I owe it to myself, and my continued career and aspirations, to know how to earn money, survive with it and hopefully save enough to live comfortably. Not only does that require education, but I must also comprehend these systems so I can criticise and advocate against them.

In the current cost-of-living crisis, being able to openly talk about money with the people in my life has been the best step in learning how to keep it. In a piece for *The Atlantic*, journalist Joe Pinsker argues that taboos around money are designed to ensure we are isolated from the system that hurts us:

> … taboos around money – among haves and have-nots alike – exert a sort of stabilizing force, blurring how much people actually have and giving them one fewer reason to be upset with their place in society.

Money is not a measure of our worth, but it is our safety net in a capitalist society. Feminism is firmly steeped in a class system, one that aims to uplift all people but too often leaves marginalised, blue-collar and women of lower classes behind. Every time wealthy women are open about their privilege, and each time women are vulnerable with their financial struggles, we move closer to a social discussion that refuses to equate money with worth. We engage in a process of connection through learning and authenticity. Our honesty, our acknowledgement of context and our conversational capacity combine as a driver for change. The resentment, the anger and the disdain I have for wealthy individuals isn't helpful if not channelled into something more: a dialogue about wealth inequality. Instead of hate-scrolling the mega-rich, I need to challenge the systems and policies that enable them. That starts with talking.

5
friendship

taboo 8:

✖

Subjects Aren't Taboo: Women's Story-Sharing Is

My grandmothers remind me of the Rest Super ad. I'm unsure if that's a nationwide or niche reference, but I think you know the one. Same age, same income, same super contribution: the difference? Cue the escalators or staircases highlighting the long-term differences in their financial outcomes. I don't think my grannies, Susan and Marlene, are comparable to financial retirement policies, but I think they represent two sides of a coin.

um – Susan – and my dad's mum – Marlene –
s. They were also both left to raise children
and they both eventually left their husbands
poor treatment. One lived a life of wealth and
of homemaking, having been forced to give up her career for
a man whose expectation was that she served him. The other
raised five children while her husband was away with the navy;
he'd come home drunk and beat her in front of my dad and
his siblings. Both my grandmothers pushed on, putting their
children first until the world changed enough for them to leave
these relationships. Their personalities, their communication
styles and their homes could not have been more different,
but they both loved card games, crime shows and making
inappropriate comments.

My gran and nan met me when I was less than sixty
minutes old. As a little girl, my understanding of my grandmas
was summed up in one word: smart. Every crossword, puzzle,
board game and chapter book was bought and mailed to me.
Marlene lived, for my primary schooling years, in a caravan
park five minutes from my house. Every three days she would
bring over a lamington sponge cake with jam and cream and a
new book I should try. By the time I was ten, Nan was banned
from giving me any books without Mum and Dad seeing them
first. She had given me a copy of a book on the Snowtown
murders, colloquially known as the 'bodies in the barrels' serial
killings, in South Australia. My parents discovered I had been

making my way through these texts when I approached Dad after school one Wednesday afternoon, the pertinent page held open with my fluffy purple bookmark, to ask him what the word 'sodomised' meant. That was a great phone call to listen in on through the study wall of our house.

I realise this isn't funny to most people, but anyone who knew my nan and me found this hysterical. When she died, this was a story my dad and aunty told in her eulogy. She just treated me like a small adult, a sponge who wanted to understand everything I came into contact with. Nan died last year, and we hadn't been close in her last few years. She never got to read my book, which she would have loved and not agreed with most of. My nan was whip-smart and vulgar, which is part of the reason I am, too.

My gran Susan is well into her eighties and works as a tour guide at the Art Gallery of New South Wales. She lives in a wealthy suburban area and doesn't leave the house without her signature L'Oréal lipstick. Everyone knows her and everyone loves her: she is the most positive person you will ever meet, which makes her absolutely insufferable to be around. The sun truly does shine out of her arse – it's exhausting. She hosts morning-tea fundraisers and wears enough hairspray to tranquilise a small horse. As a six-year-old, I begged Mum and Dad to let me go on trips alone to stay with her for a week in Melbourne (she lived there with her partner at the time). Straight off the plane we would drive to a bookshop and pick up something that fascinated me. In the space of six days Gran bought me every Judy Moody book I could get my paws on. Suse would think 'suck' is crass, but no longer flinches when I say 'fuck' three times a sentence. She gives every one of her friends a copy of my book even though most of them have voted Liberal for the last seven decades without fail. She texts me with eighteen irrelevant emojis at the tail end of every blue iPhone bubble: *My friend gave your book back and said it's not for her. I suppose she is ninety-four. Love always, Your Granny* typed out directly underneath her name, phone number and profile picture.

I imagine her giggling as she puts the book in the mail for another friend, before breaking into the chesty cough that will never quite go away.

My grandmothers are two of the most exceptional women I know. They were my first friends. Women of the same era, but different classes. What we had in common was books, cake and intellect. They were interested in the world; they were interested in knowing things and talking about them with me. I never truly appreciated them for this: for how different they were, and for how they socialised me. They accepted, loved and cherished me without condition. This fact has stuck with me in recent years. I never truly understood these women who pushed me academically, who have hurt me, who love me, who have offended me and who are complex in all the ways women are. This is because for a long time I could not digest that they did not always agree with or understand my decisions or the way I lived my life.

'I have choices now that you didn't have,' I would bash on every time they challenged my view on something (usually my will to get drunk and wear short dresses out every weekend).

But I had articulated the crux of the conflict within my frustration. As choices become available to women, as we are compelled to speak up about all the issues we face, it feels to me like older women were too often silent and subservient. I would judge them: they just 'didn't understand me'. To older women, I assume it can feel horrific that younger generations complain about lifestyles, opportunities and experiences that they never even had. Every single day I whinge about the side effects of a pill they didn't have access to. I complain about hook-up culture, which they could never even contemplate participating in. I don't want to work too hard; they wish they could have kept their jobs or even had their own bank accounts to be paid into. I see the taboo as the issue. That they were expected to remain silent, to be resilient in the face of oppression. I find this conversation most interesting, because it walks the line between 'honest' and 'too honest'. I've had friends' mums say they wouldn't describe childbirth accurately in order not to 'scare us off', or, worse, denigrating those complaining with the old adage of 'it isn't that bad' when presented with the reality of having sex with someone who doesn't look at you, let alone pleasure you. I am grateful for the fights of the women

ut their ability to suffer in silence is a symptom of

many are still sick with. They shouldn't have had

to get on with it' but that doesn't mean that I should, too.

When it came to my grandmas, the women who gave me every book and let me ask every question under the sun, it was always interesting that their political, feminist and social views didn't always align with this messaging. They were proud of me, and they wanted me to have options and freedoms to choose from. When it came to their own lives, they remained conservative. What I once saw as a regressive state, I now understand is true love. My grandmas love me without always understanding me. It's probably why I wept during *Barbie* when Ruth said, 'We mothers stand still so our daughters can look back and see how far they've come.' My grandmas talked to me about everything under the sun, and with this, they ensured I would never be silent in all the ways they had to be.

X

When you think of the word 'gossip', what image is conjured in your mind? Honestly, I see women whispering. I hear murmurs and giggles. I see the mums of girls at my primary school saying awful things about me. I feel the glare of a table as I walk past. I see a pack of year-nine girls I'm terrified to walk past in the street (does that fear ever go away?). Gossip is equated with women. It is the language of the nasty. It implies negative judgement, inaccuracy and drama.

But what is gossip? The word 'gossip' originated from Old English 'godsibb' which meant a sponsor or godparent. It essentially described a sibling from God, and was then extended to mean a close friend – specifically, women who were invited to attend a birth – by the 14th century. By the 16th century 'gossip' was born, meaning to talk about people we know.

Fascinating though that it is actually a word that historically referred to close female friendships. The subsequent definition of the word is, you guessed it, a patriarchal imposition. Despite the present-day understanding and the negative connotations embedded deep into my socially conditioned skull, I believe gossip is making a comeback. It's undergone a period of reputation rehab, a moment, a reformation. I've seen ticketed panels on the topic, read articles on its morality and have begun to firmly believe and better understand it as a vital function of connection.

Often, shared criticism is more bonding than shared positivity. If you're 'tut-tutting', get fucking real. We all do it: you're not above it. The question is, where is the line between neutral social chatter, healthy criticism and problematic and directed hatred? Writer Alice Porter elucidates this in her piece 'Gossiping isn't frivolous or immoral – I love it'. Porter explains that traditionally gossip was perceived as something done by women and that its defamatory public perception is man-made. In the 17th century, the meaning of the word changed to the commonly understood current definition: 'someone who engages in "idle talk" and the sharing of secrets'. But Porter articulates that it was simultaneously during this period that gossip was tied to immorality in women. Female friendships were a target of the witch hunts, thus the language of gossip earned an unethical association. In 1547, gossip was actually a punishable offence: it was forbidden for 'women to meet together to babble and talk'. Conversation became the threat: women's discussions and information-sharing were criminal actions. The patriarchal enforcement of this ruling was with a scold's bridle. Porter writes: 'According to the BBC, this was a "bizarre form of punishment reserved exclusively for women" whereby a metal, muzzle-style cage was placed over the head, forcing a spike into the wearer's mouth to stop them speaking.'

In a video that has been liked more than four million times, TikTok creator Lara Kelly references Rose-Aimeé Bélanger's statue *The Gossipers*, a bronze depiction of three women conversing. In the video, Kelly confirms that the term 'gossip' originally referred to close friendships and that its misogynistic modern application has transformed its original meaning to apply judgement and stigma to women's conversations about the social behaviour we experience. Women speaking to each other is threatening to patriarchy. Laws requiring obedience, submission and the punishing of our conversations have stigmatised centuries of close relationships between women and the thoughts and perspectives we share.

Again: men engage in gossip as frequently as women, but only women are socially punished for the act.

While we know it often can be, gossip isn't just 'bitching' about someone. Think about that sentence – the colloquial description of the act itself. 'Talking about someone', 'critiquing someone' and 'speaking candidly about an experience or perception of someone' do not carry the same gendered emphasis, the same vulgarity as 'bitching'. Because the image that entered your mind was likely shrill, sour and nasty. The language we use to discuss women's opinions is significantly more toxic. Our language alters our perception of the world, and over time we have plastered social and cultural imagery on the surface of every mind, to ensure female acts are always seen as more dangerous, more problematic and more shameful.

Gossip is broader than the negative discussion of a person. Suspend the beliefs you have. Think of how gossiping covers social networks, changes in relational dynamics, storytelling and personal reflection. When we gossip aren't we ultimately just sharing our inner worlds and contemplations with those we trust? Calling a girl a slag isn't the gossip I'm advocating, but consulting with a trusted source that you have concerns a friend's relationship is displaying signs of coercive control would, in the eyes of much of society, also fit under that same terminology. For many it is still an opportunity to indulge in the shaming of others, but what if we expanded our view to understand that this form of communication is vital to our human experience?

Gossip teaches me what my friends think about their relationships, their workplace dynamics, their failures and their ambitions. It is insight into their emotional states. I reflect on my own behaviours and how they compare to the criticisms women close to me have of others in their lives. I am able to observe, consciously and subconsciously, social behavioural patterns and expectations and gauge where I sit within these categories. I evolve my political views and my ability to empathise through these processes. Gossip doesn't need to end: it needs a moral standard and a rebrand. The art of gossip is central to the dismantling of taboo. When we speak, we dismantle fears and shame around socially prescribed ways of being. We acquire safe spaces that encourage honest articulations of the human experience. It is a measure of social health.

When we shame women's friendships as frivolous, shallow and mean-spirited, we socially proscribe those relationships as immoral or inferior to romantic partnerships, working relationships and familial structures. Women's stories are taboo, and valuing and elevating the status of our friendships is, too. Understanding this is the key to unpacking and altering our relational hierarchies. Friendship is our most influential social force, and I believe it is the only relationship we actively, consistently choose without cultural constraint or pressure.

taboo 9:

✕

Friendships Are More Powerful Than Romantic Relationships

'If there is one singular factor that predicts your psychological health and wellbeing, your physical health and wellbeing, and even how long you live, it is the number and quality of close friendships that you have.'

The statement above was delivered by Robin Dunbar, a professor of evolutionary psychology at the University of

Oxford, a Fellow of the British Academy for the humanities and social sciences, and arguably the most prominent academic working in the study of human friendships.

Finally, our social views are catching up to the known data. In 2023, *The Washington Post* published an article stating that 55 per cent of gen Z and millennials now say friendship is more important than a romantic relationship. In 2020, an Oxford study evidenced that both men and women report higher levels of intimacy with their best friends than their romantic partners. Is our relationship hierarchy changing? Are we only now recognising the unique value provided by our platonic relationships? Or are young people just better positioned to value friendships while we have more time and capacity for broad socialisation? Is this an act of cognitive dissonance, where we value our friendships mentally but do not act on these beliefs publicly?

What has come to be known as Dunbar's number contends that humans are only cognitively able to maintain about 150 connections at once. More recent data suggests this number is higher. That sounds fucking exhausting, and I say that as a high-functioning extrovert. Dunbar's inner-circle recommendation, though, is that people should have about five close friends and a larger outer layer of more casual connections. In an article for *The Guardian*, writer Emma Beddington frames Dunbar's central thesis:

We become friends with one another because there is something we like and have in common with someone: this is homophily, or the 'birds of a feather' phenomenon. 'These are relationships that are seen as "clicking" from the start,' says Robin Dunbar, an emeritus professor of evolutionary psychology at the University of Oxford. Dunbar defines the 'seven pillars of friendship' as similarities that predispose people to become friends: language or dialect, geography, educational experiences, hobbies and interests, moral or spiritual viewpoints, political views, sense of humour and taste in music.

This information isn't particularly shocking. We connect with people through shared experiences, interests and viewpoints. But knowing the number of close friends and casual friendships we have capacity for, and should ideally have, begs further questions. When and why do we experience declines in the number of friends we have and the quality and depth of these connections?

A 2017 study undertaken in the Netherlands looked at how the age at which people decided to become parents impacted their personal relationships. The conclusion was simple: the strength and quality of friendships decreases after people become parents. The more specific and surprising element was at what age of the child this tends to occur: three. It may not be that generation Z and millennials surveyed about friendship actually see it as having more value than older generations do, but that, as we more frequently see people choosing to have fewer children, no children or children later in life, our perception of friendship remains elevated for years longer. Have we just not reached the drop-off point yet?

A 2016 study by scientists from Aalto University in Finland and the University of Oxford found that our social circles shrink after the age of twenty-five. (Again I wonder, will these trends change as our social norms do?) This number was calculated by analysing the mobile phone data of three million people to determine the patterns of our contact and our overall social activity. Unsurprisingly, there was a gendered divide in our social networking behavioural patterns. The average twenty-five-year-old woman contacted 17.5 people each month, whereas men contacted nineteen people. This number declines for the rest of our lives, the data showed.

I argue our digital footprint, however, is not an adequate indicator of friendship quality or the satisfaction levels we feel with these connections. Women are more likely to engage in deeper, long-term friendships with other women, while men may have larger networks that offer more shallow opportunities for social interaction. Our nation's data on loneliness speaks to this reality. The Australian Institute of Health and Welfare defines loneliness as a 'subjective unpleasant or distressing feeling of a lack of connection to other people, along with a desire for more, or more satisfying, social relationships'. It is fundamentally different from 'being alone'.

According to the 2023 Ending Loneliness Together report, Australians who feel lonely are four times more likely to have a chronic disease, 4.6 times more likely to have depression and 4.6 times more likely to have social anxiety. While in 2023 Australian studies concluded that almost one-third of the population reported feeling lonely, we know this disproportionately affects men. A 2023 survey conducted by Healthy Male, a men's health organisation, uncovered that 43 per cent of Australian men were lonely. While many of us believe loneliness is most often experienced by elderly people, the data indicated that men aged thirty-five to forty-nine experienced the highest levels of loneliness. Experiencing loneliness is not an indicator that a person does not have friends, but that those friendships lack the quality of connection required to meet social satisfaction. A 2010 study by professor of psychology and neuroscience at Brigham Young University in Utah Julianne Holt-Lunstad determined that loneliness is as harmful to our health as smoking fifteen cigarettes each day. We know that our relationships are vital to our health, and we know we experience a decline after the first quarter of our lives. Our friendships evolve and change over time, as do all our relationships. But how can we see them through these processes?

My high-school best friend, Claudia, remains one of my closest friends today. Through complex family dynamics, mental-health conditions, parental divorces, interstate and overseas moves and career transitions, we'd been through more together by the age of nineteen than some friends have by forty. Claudia is the best friend I know to everyone she encounters. I love her and believe she is the kindest person on earth. I also find her effort exhausting to be around, because her presence in individual and group dynamics makes me feel insecure as a friend. It doesn't get more honest than that. She always has flowers, baked goods and too much time on her hands to spend on other people. For years, I struggled to believe her excessive thoughtfulness could possibly be authentic. That sounds totally evil, but it's true. Do you know someone who just oozes joy and wants to be around people at all times? Instead of sitting in their presence and warmth, it feels like a mirror being held up to you with *YOU ARE A SELFISH MOLE: BE MORE LIKE CLAUDIA* written in ink across your forehead.

For most of our friendship, this dynamic hasn't been healthy. It involved a power imbalance, where Claudia was trying much harder in our relationship than I was. It was often a big sister, little sister dynamic. Claudia followed me around, and I would use this power and then reject her when I wanted to be alone. I loved her, but I was also using her because I knew she was a good friend. When I felt smothered by this love, as a child who didn't like intense affection or emotion, I would simply put up a brick wall. It's logical, basic human power dynamics: the more you try to push yourself onto someone, the harder they are going to pull away. I understand that these behaviours

I was engaging in are a form of bullying. When someone tries to make themselves heard and they are met with silence, you teach them that objecting to poor treatment and voicing their emotions means they will be discarded. You re-enforce their submission. I think about this a lot: I am disgusted by it and disappointed in myself that it took me so long to learn this.

When we graduated high school and I moved to Queensland, our relationship flourished. Long-distance friendship meant we could give each other space, equal opportunity for communication and effort, and we had new boundaries and parameters for our friendship. We would FaceTime for a couple of hours every few months, we would make annual trips and stay with each other, we had clear lines of communication. Claudia and I thrived because we missed each other. Fast forward to me returning to New South Wales and to us living in the same city, Sydney, for the first time in five years. Suddenly, the dynamic shifted. We were engaging in a push/pull dynamic where our expectations, communication styles and priorities were not aligned. We were our seventeen-year-old selves again. I was constantly disappointing her, and Claudia was constantly responding by doing more and more to attempt to get me to do exactly what she wanted without hearing or accepting my boundaries or needs.

When I asked for scheduled quality time on a Sunday, she would turn up at my door unannounced on a Tuesday with flowers and cake. It was distressing, seeing my friend spend money and time on me in a way that I couldn't appreciate. She wanted to feel a sense of control in our relationship; she wanted to tell me she was here for me and that these were the friendship parameters she wanted. In contrast, what I wanted was to get back in control of my own life in a new city, with a new business and a new living arrangement. There was a disconnect between us, and it was hurting both of us. There isn't a single thing she does not know about me. There isn't a single thing I do not know about her. Our issue was not one of awareness, it was that we were yelling our needs, but they were at odds. There had been no understanding and no compromise. I couldn't escape the guilt that Claudia was constantly there for me, but I couldn't provide her with the intense emotional closeness she required. Friendship must know its bounds. It has layers and facets. A friend understands and appreciates the different versions of you: past, present and future. These platonic romances are not about blind loyalty: they are about fostering the safety to admit to failure with the expectation that you will need to do better in future.

Over a three-month period, we clearly communicated what our needs were and how we could each compromise to engage in a better flow into the future of our love. I was going to lead conversations and make plans actively instead of avoiding commitment, and Claudia was going to stop video calling me three times a day and start doing voice notes instead. There is obviously a lot more to it, but these were the small movements we could engage in that made a big impact in our relationship.

Then, two weeks before she left to move overseas for two years, Claudia called me, crying.

'I just wanted to say I am sorry.'

'What the fuck is going on? Sorry for what? Are we still getting Thai?' I had been thinking about my Pad See Ew for days.

'For thinking that forcing friendship in the way I wanted it on you was friendship.'

Holy shit.

'I was not listening to what you actually needed from me as a friend – I was just overdoing it and then getting upset with you for telling me you just wanted to spend time with me.'

'I'm sorry for being so poor with my communication and so avoidant of conflict. I have been a terrible friend to you, and you've been nothing but there for me.'

We cried for at least an hour, obviously. Then we booked accommodation for Christmas together in Europe where she would be living. Claudia is my family. She is one of my platonic life partners. I know, deeply, that we will be old women together. I understand this because since I was thirteen we have been able to see, hear and know each other at a level I have never experienced with a romantic partner. Women do not need sex to connect with each other. We just need time, thought and communication. Even after a year of tough friendship, we did not want to break up. Friendship breakups are far worse than romantic ones in my opinion – because love between women exists at a different wavelength. I think about former friends ten times more often than ex-partners. Romantic relationships run their course, but friendships can be a forever connection that comes in and out of our lives, adapting to circumstance. When these break down, it feels unnecessary and it wounds like the most personal of attacks. It isn't about appearance or sex or children or life partnership – it feels like a more personal rejection of womanhood.

I will never stop arguing that female friendships are the deepest of our lives. If we compared heterosexual romantic relationships to friendships, more people would be single. Our standards would be far higher.

what can we learn from friendship that would enhance romantic relationships

That love does not scream or slam doors or leave when things are hard. That love changes and evolves as a person does. That our closeness is not dependent on sex or touch. That love notices the mood changes and hormonal signals and packs snacks accordingly. It's keeping important deadlines and stressful family moments in their calendars just as a reminder to check in. Love celebrates you beyond your birthday and Christmas. Love is letting go of the belief that your relationship will always look the same, lowering expectations when circumstances change and having the awareness and security to know it isn't always about you. It is helping draft the message, and it is catching the phone they throw away from themselves because they need to pretend technology doesn't exist after telling a boy they'd like to go out for a drink this Friday when they actually mean 'I've had a crush on you for years and I'd like to have sex with you in a sundress on a Saturday afternoon.' Love is buying them tickets to that thing they mentioned seven months ago just because and making a shared playlist and giving them the last hot chip and telling them their other flare pants are the better choice for the party. Love is giving a huge fuck. It is noticing. It is listening. It is remembering. Love is the awareness women give to each other's emotional states. It is walking arm in arm covered in glitter through the concert gates and it is commenting *SLAY* on the photo you approved out of the seventy-eight you reviewed. Love is getting coffee and grabbing an extra pastry on the way over. Love is thinking of them just because why wouldn't you, they are brilliant. Women take up more space in each other's minds than we are allowed to physically occupy in public spaces. Friendship is building an IKEA cabinet with your best friends on the floor of your new house in your pyjamas and one taking a break from her Allen key to declare that not wearing undies is fun until you start discharging down your leg. It is calling them a skank or a mole or a slag or feral when they use your good face cream when actually what you really mean is that they are the most brilliant, exceptional, radiant energy to grace the earth and you hope that when you're ninety-seven you'll still order deep pan pizzas, have glasses of red and lay shit on the guys who didn't deserve you in the first place. It does not shame: it allows you to flourish. Friendship is hard conversations, hearing criticism and adapting accordingly. It is eighty-seven funny videos that are just our niche brand of humour (probably liked and shared by three million other women) in your unread messages. It's holding you to account for bad behaviour and continuing to love you, not overlooking it. Love is wanting to be exactly like other girls. In Conversations on Love, Natasha Lunn writes, 'Love is not a state of enthusiasm. It is a verb. It implies action, demonstration, ritual, practices, communication, expression. It is the ability to take responsibility for one's own behaviour. Responsibility is freedom.'

On an episode of *The Imperfects* podcast, the show's regular guest psychologist, Dr Emily Musgrove, introduced the term 'mimetic desire'. Mimetic desire, a concept first articulated by French philosopher René Girard, suggests that our desires are driven by the desires of others, or what they already have. Basically, we want what others want and we want what others already have. The argument follows that it is then impossible to know what we truly want in this world because we are following a prescribed model influenced by the people around us. If everyone is getting married, having kids and buying a house they can't afford, most people are trying to measure up to that same standard.

Authors of a 2013 journal paper, 'Sliding versus Deciding in Relationships: Associations with Relationship Quality, Commitment, and Infidelity', examined how purposeful decision-making within interpersonal relationships, as opposed to sliding through life and relational transitions, led to higher quality relationships and lowered personal stress. The paper used a sample of 252 men and women, and the results showed that regardless of relationship status (whether the surveyed individuals were dating, cohabiting or married), those who reported more thoughtful decision-making processes also reported more dedication to their partners, higher satisfaction with the relationship, and fewer 'extradyadic involvements' (cough, cheating). We anecdotally know this about relationships, as we watch people move in with a partner for convenience and obey what they see as a biological necessity to have children – and often just fall through their lives not wanting to disrupt the status quo. Subversion is scary.

What then, does a system of patriarchy enforce us to mimic? Do we actually desire marriage, or has the wedding industrial complex imposed the view that we each deeply want to spend $50,000 on a white dress, a shitload of alcohol and a fun party in order to be contractually tied to each other in a religious ceremony registered to a government department? Without getting into a debate about free will and human agency, how can we discern what we want when all we have known is a system built to benefit men?

I think friendship is healthy because it is the thing that escapes mimetic desire. We don't make and celebrate friends because those relationships are something we believe we should have. We search out female friendship in its highest quality because it sustains us. It is purposeful connection. I have never felt that a single friendship I have had has 'slid' into my life or out of control, it has always been a purposeful action. When I have lost friends, that has been a choice – but at no point have we slid out without one party actively choosing to no longer maintain the connection.

Do you ever hear some 'tragic' story over coffee with a friend where they gasp that a relative or colleague has just called off an engagement or got an early divorce? I always find that exciting. To hear someone has stopped sliding through their life, has chosen pain and difficulty and circumvented what they know was coming in a few decades? It is that moment when someone has thought to the end of their life, pictured the regret of staying exactly as they are now – unmoving – and decided that it's worth an immediate explosion to get their life back. They are more afraid of remaining in an average predicament for their entire life than causing a major inconvenience. To me, it is the sound of scissors cutting through fabric at the Spotlight counter. It's tearing through relationships and drawing a distinct line between the life you have and the life you know you want for yourself, despite not actually knowing how it will feel or if it will eventuate. It is taking the risk because walking the prescribed path is committing yourself to a dull hum in the back of your mind forever, telling you that it could have been better, you would not be so miserable, if only you had just …

Dolly Alderton wrote, 'Everything I know about love I've learnt from my long-term female friendships.' There's a reason this resonated with millions of girls around the world. While I am destined to fall into some of the patterns set by my parents, my childhood context and the people around me I love and admire, I believe I am more likely to be influenced in my life decisions by friends. I do not slide into friendships, but do I align my decision-making, or at the very least my timing, with my close community's life choices and stages? If friendships influence our decisions and are the single biggest predictor of our long-term health and wellbeing, who we choose to love and how we love them are the most important considerations of our lives.

In *All About Love*, feminist writer bell hooks articulates the concept of cathexis. She asserts that when we feel deeply drawn to someone, we 'cathect' them: investing our feelings and emotions in them. She argues that most people confuse this act, of making someone the object of our affection, with the act of loving. hooks advances this concept, observing how individuals who cathect believe and claim to love people they hurt, abuse and neglect. They verbally enforce this as love. However, hooks says those who engage in this behaviour are not capable of loving us, if our understanding of love is that it is to nurture our own and another's spiritual growth.

My choice to love and nurture my female friendships escapes the sliding and requires deciding. While some people would have experienced friendship that isn't love, but acts of cathexis, I believe loving women is an active choice I make every day. Who I choose to love and how is not something that is monitored and judged in the ways that my career, my body and my romantic relationships are. When the friends you choose do not follow the pathways of submission but actively discuss and challenge taboos, you have alternate examples of the life women can lead. There is no clearer subversion of the notion of 'falling' in love than choosing to engage and centre women in your life who challenge the status quo and encourage you to do the same.

The private conversations women have and how we influence each other to lead shame-free lives will change the world. Perhaps this is just an alternate form of mimetic desire, but I would choose it every time. My friends are not objects of affection: we are participants in each other's continual evolution. Friendship has always been, and will always be, the most intentional act of my life. It's not driven by spontaneous desire or social conditions that tell me at all times I must love, must fuck and must work. Friendship, to me, is the enjoyment of another individual's personhood. It is getting to observe their navigation of life and opting to partake in both the chaos and the calm.

When I was reading material on female friendships, the first search results proved one of the central issues in the valuation and centring of female friendship. *The Guardian* came in first, with 'Why do female friendships fizzle out?', then 'The Complexities of Female Friendship' and 'How to Navigate Female Friendships'; followed by *The Times* and *The Atlantic* rounding out the top five with 'Why female friendship is the most difficult relationship of all' and 'Why Women's Friendships Are So Complicated'. In a society that has sidelined female friendship, demoting it to a tier below career, family and partner, the remnants of whatever time women have left are dedicated to managing the administrative load and attempting to reclaim any time back for our own health. Our friendships are most likely to fizzle due to our unavailability.

Taboo

My mum and dad do not have close friends they see consistently; I can't name three of their friends they see more than monthly. Growing up in a working-class family, I watched my parents spend decades unhappily committed to building a family and working full-time to pay off a mortgage in an economic climate they could not afford. Their friendships had to be convenient – mostly colleagues or the parents of other kids – and I rarely saw my mum or dad individually take a few hours out of their day for a friend. It was a family barbecue, not a one-on-one coffee. I often think about how childfree people feel during these times, knowing they have lost friends to a commitment they do not have. I can only assume that all parties feel isolated, and long to see and connect with their friends as people again.

Female friendship specifically has been sidelined to romantic love, to childrearing and to our careers. Most women with a healthy circle of female friends know it is the most replenishing, restorative part of our lives. Patriarchy hates that and sells you that it is the problem. This is internalised misogyny at play, creating the false notion that women are difficult to navigate, relate to and have relationships with. All relationships require compromise, understanding and the ability to change. These are inherent facts of life. What differentiates friendship from romantic partnerships is the way in which it occupies our mental space. We find it easier to discard and deprioritise friendship because work, romantic partnership and children are seen as the more immediate priorities. Friendship is positioned as an outlet for venting and 'taking a break' from these central pieces of our personal puzzle. We build a life and friendship is told to 'slot in' where it can.

But when I asked my mum about her own experience of friendship amid motherhood, work and marriage, she actively disagreed with me.

'Actually, I made lots of friends when you were young. Through mothers' groups for newborns and then at school. These communities were fantastic support networks. Divorce was the thing that isolated me. I lost most of my female friends. It felt to me that women either didn't know how to deal with a single woman or they chose a side. The narrative is built and it is hard to break through when you make couple friends as a couple. Since then I have found it very difficult to make new friends but I don't have many. I found it hurtful and difficult to trust people when the women in my life told me to take him back. When I didn't, I was alienated. I now meet lots of women I would like to pursue friendships with through business, [but] being self-employed means I am often time poor still.'

My assumption that the hardest years of my mum's life were early motherhood and work were wrong. I had always seen that, when she made the choice to leave her marriage, it was hard but ultimately recalibrated her life. I had never bothered to ask this question before, and never knew this was more isolating than becoming a mum itself. The very thing that undid my mother's friendships, in her eyes, was not the balance of work and children, but the impact of a relationship breakdown. The continued social centring of romantic partnerships was an experience of exclusion.

My partner should be one of my closest friends, but they shouldn't outrank or be labelled my best friend. The relationship is distinct in expression of intimacy, but romance is not more important than friendship. They are different. Our female friendships are the key to dismantling shame, to unlearning the stigma that comes with women's subjects. I've never once been alone in my life. Not when I've sat in the carpark of a McDonald's with a strawberry thickshake in my pyjamas with my roommates after a bad work week, not when I've been sent twenty-seven voice notes and videos by my best friend living overseas, who likes to provide me with the sitcom of her life to ensure we do not miss a beat. Not even in book-writing, the most solitary of acts, when my best friend comes off her fourth twelve-hour paramedic shift and says, 'I've meal prepped you a lasagna and a pumpkin soup; no disordered eating while book-writing.'

I have always made friends easily: it is the greatest privilege of all. I have never once had to worry about struggling to meet people or keep up conversation, because I am unafraid of failing. While dating is a cocktail of anxiety and insecurity, women are a safety net. In all the changes in our social conditions and experiences of feminism, I see friendship as the common thread. Female friendship is a force that can transcend age, class, religion, education, race and beyond. This is not taboo – it is undervalued. The true taboo of female friendship is to acknowledge that it is far more powerful than our romantic relationships. It isn't appreciated or understood for what it is. As I enter the period in which research tells me my platonic relationships will steadily decline, I want to continue to interrogate what it actually means to be a friend, and what feeling I want to invoke and feel in all my social connections.

how to make and maintain high-quality friendships as an adult

1. Treat making friends like dating, because, in fact, cultivating quality friendships is far more important to your health and long-term wellbeing than dating. Here's how:

   - Ask them out. If you want to make friends, you have to make a move. Whether it be a colleague, someone you've met through social sport or a friend of a friend you really want to call your own – send them a text or ask them to get a coffee next week at X cafe at X time. Go after what you want, and make the plan. Rejection is the worst thing that can happen.

   - Send a follow-up text, send them something funny, start the chain of communication and feel out what works best for that person. Just because someone does not text does not mean they do not care; they might be a voice-note, phone-call or meme-dump friend. Find what works and communicate accordingly.

   - Always follow through. Consider venues and activities they would like, make the booking, get there early. No one likes a flake.

2. Know what kind of friend you are. Identify what kind of friendship you are after. Where does it sit in the layers of closeness? Are you looking for a casual friend or a close one? How do you establish connection with a person? Do you need an activity? Are you a weekly check-in or a biannual kind of person? You need to understand how you show up, and what that person wants from your friendship. Those things need to align or a compromise needs to be reached. This requires ongoing communication. Sometimes someone will like you more than you like them and vice versa. It's like dating, and you need to work out how you feel and assert clear boundaries when gaps arise.

3. If you're struggling to make different kinds of friends, the best suggestion I have is volunteering somewhere. If there's a skill you want to develop, a course you want to take or a hobby you want to try, volunteering a couple of hours a week at a charity or starting a class is the best way to make friends who aren't already within your echo chamber. Sign up to a social sport. A walking club. A hobby group. Find an outlet that makes you feel most comfortable to chat, and go at least three times. Deep breath: the long-term outcome is worth the short-term 'I want to be swallowed by the earth' feeling. If your high-school friends suck and you have no common ground,

don't go back there. You need to branch out. Fewer friends with more satisfaction are ultimately better than more lower-quality connections.

4. If you are finding issues with your current friends, consider what parts of your context they are from. Is it possible your group are all your university college friends that you'd get pissed and vomit at a bus stop with? Are they all from the same city? Do you have a group or one-on-one friends? Consider the pattern of dynamics at play and whether you engage with a diverse group of people. Every single one of my close friends has moved cities, most have different career paths and many entered at different points in my life. These experiences bring texture and emotional intelligence to my relationships. They show me what's working and what isn't functional. I get different things from different people. We have different gossip points, interest areas and careers to agonise over. I exist in a kaleidoscope of perspectives: it makes my life brilliant (not to brag, but also absolutely to brag).

5. Keep a list of talking points in your Notes app. This is my favourite thing to bring to any interaction with a friend. During the week I make a list of things that have happened that I want to share, and content I've watched or things I've learned that I would like to discuss.

I plan talking points for walks, coffee dates, weekends away and long drives. Comfortable silence is great, but sometimes we want to chit chat and have forgotten what has happened to us and how we have been feeling recently. Social anxiety can take over. My Notes app is a diary, a summary of interesting thoughts. I refuse to be mocked for this; it makes every interaction more exciting. Yes, sometimes I read them back after a dream and it says 'Why did Ariel trade her voice for legs, Eric only had nice hair', but mostly it's good shit.

6. Find what setting works best for your friend. You can and should test expansions of the friendship, but often one dynamic works best. Some friends are better side-by-side friends (people you do exercise classes with, or attend a comedy show or sports game to sit alongside), others are for group experiences and some thrive in one-on-one dinners and drinks.

7. If you only drink alcohol with your friend, are they someone you actually like being around? Or is your friendship built on enabling lowered inhibitions as a form of coping?

8. If you do not feel you can communicate with your friend and give honest feedback without fear of a fight, they are not your friend.

9. The perfect friendship is one that knows its parameters.

10. There are friends you can live with, but not travel with. There are friends you get coffee and work out with, but you would never take them on a group weekend away. There are friends you level with politically, and friends who are great in a changeroom mental breakdown scenario and who explain to you who Olivia Rodrigo is. Sometimes, there are friends you want to scroll with in silence (a Cheek follower coined this 'cage time') on a hungover Sunday, who expect nothing of you except the occasional toe touch and an Uber Eats order from KFC. There are others you want to go into business with. These friendships are not 'better' or 'worse' than others, they allow you to access different parts of yourself in healthy ways.

11. Friendship is the most powerful force in the world. Prioritise it.

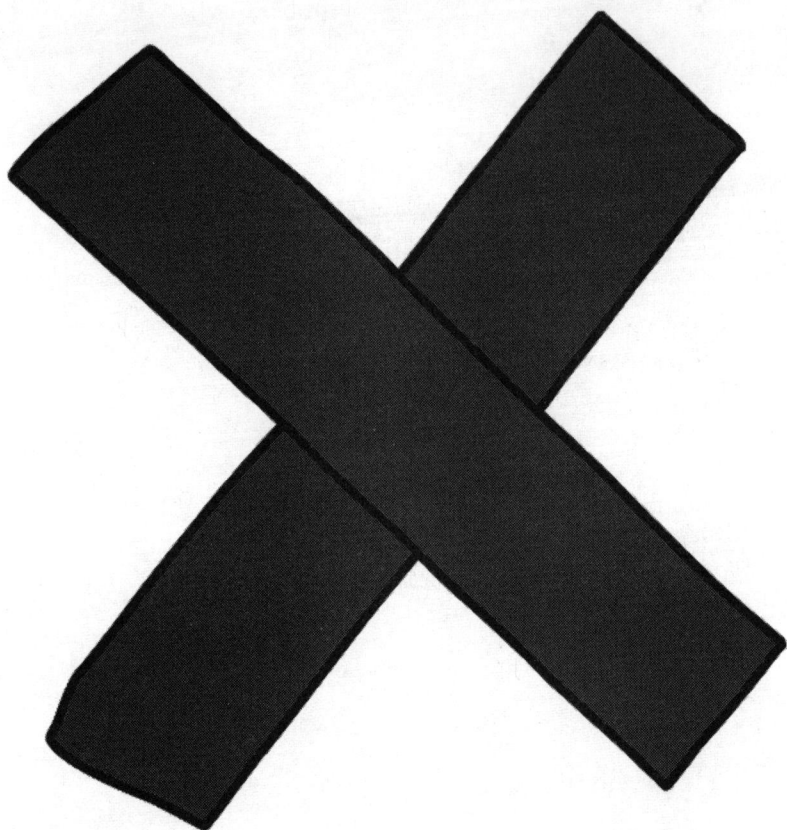

conclusion

Earlier this year during a session with my psychologist I was ruminating on some confusion I was having in relation to my work. I was trying to describe the emotions I was feeling, but essentially I was worried that if things kept going well with my career I would 'lose touch' with parts of myself. She asked me to explain what I meant, and I struggled to articulate the issue beyond a prospective fear. Softly she told me: 'I think you've shed a lot of self-doubt and shame in the last year. You don't know what to do with all the new emotional space you have without it.'

Don't you love when mental-health professionals deliver you a gem – something you want to lie down and stare at the ceiling thinking about for the next three to five business days? It was a compliment, but a loaded one. In the weeks before the session I had been restless, trying to find all the shame and fear I had put down. I had been working hard for the previous two years to manage my anxiety diagnosis, to get more confident speaking in public and to be comfortable occupying space and feeling pride and seeing value in the work I do. I wanted to value myself as enough without work, too. When that psychological and emotional work was paying off, it was almost like I wanted my pain back. It was familiar. I had lived with it for so long that its absence caused a new wave of confusion that I tried to create narratives to justify. The story I told myself was that being happy and mentally well was disconnecting me from my mission. I firmly believed my shame was part of me and that my pain made me a better writer, a more relatable person and a harder-working young woman. If I didn't hate myself, what did that mean for my drive to impress people, to achieve and to speak to relatable personal experiences?

I knew intellectually these thoughts were absurd, but they lived in my body. They sat in my stomach, anchoring me to a belief that I was not worthy of true confidence and that I needed to earn approval. Likes and comments were a daily gratification ritual. Hate messages and death threats kept me grounded. If I no longer judged myself by these metrics, what would happen? The answer really is: my work got better. I am less afraid than ever of trying, of failing and of putting myself out there in new and uncomfortable ways. I am more willing to speak and to take risks than ever.

Communication has always been the antidote to shame. Speaking aloud the thing we feel makes us unlovable, flawed or a failure is a tonic. It is the first step in the restoration of the belief that we are worthy just as we are. When we communicate our fears, our untold experiences and the secrets we have kept because we believed society would not handle them with care, we free ourselves of patriarchy's binding. Telling someone you've been struggling with disordered eating, with understanding your sexuality, with the decision to get married, or to stay financially afloat is scary. We have been taught that these thoughts or experiences make us failures – fundamentally weak or inferior. They don't. They never have.

Anyone who makes you feel small for being honest about the things you struggle with is an agent of patriarchy, consciously or not. I have not written this book because I have been able to shed all the layers of shame I need to in order to share these stories. I still carry the fear, and feel the emotional exposure and risk that comes with vulnerability. Shame is still very much part of my life, despite my growth. I have no idea how many people this will resonate with, or how I may be opening myself up to judgement and backlash. I write about the things that make me uncomfortable because I believe being honest, putting myself out there and doing it scared will ultimately get me much further in life than standing firmly, sheltered in the crowd of people committed to reinforcing a culture of silence.

The points at which I told someone about my fears around my own sexual violations, my work ethic and the way I was being mistreated in relationships were all before-and-after moments in a transformation of not only how I felt about the experiences I was describing, but about myself. When we read, listen to or view another person engaging in this process, relatable or not, it empowers us to do the same. While committing these stories to paper will be one of the most frightening experiences of my life, I do it selfishly. It is catharsis to stop lying to myself and others. I do it with the knowledge that no matter whether it is relatable or isolating, impactful or not, I put myself out there. I had a go. I revealed some dark parts of myself in the pursuit of connecting with people who just might feel the same. That's more than most people will ever say.

I want better for five-year-old me, for all our younger selves. The small people who absorbed information like sponges and gave freely without fear. I want to live my life in a way that makes her proud. I want to reclaim every part of her that I can. That starts simply with talking: feeling the fear and saying it anyway.

You are not going to wake up tomorrow and decide you're ready to buy one of those vibrators that looks more like a rocket ship than a sex toy if you've never engaged in solo pleasure before. When I say let's break down taboos, I'm not suggesting we start talking at work morning tea about whether Janice has tried a pulsing dildo before over a stale Anzac biscuit – there are boundaries around respectful and constructive discussions. What I am suggesting is that you shouldn't have to hide your tampon as you walk to the fucking toilet and feel terrified of someone knowing about a natural bodily process. I am arguing that people should be paid for the work they do and be able to ask for more. I want us to dedicate more time to friendship, and to discussing difficult decisions around motherhood and why we get married.

The purpose of this book is not to inspire an overnight awakening. Shame doesn't work like that. This is an invitation to question yourself. I mean that. I want you to interrogate the why behind every negative belief you've held about yourself, and the ways in which these conceal the parts of you that are important to explore. Our shame can leak into those around us, and we need to examine how our own internalised hatred can affect more than just us. We need to interrogate the people who have othered us and see with renewed insight that they too have been shut down by a fear of the taboo.

Divesting ourselves of shame and breaking free of taboos that have silenced us is a long process, but it is one with immeasurable reward. This is an opening for curiosity, for vulnerability and to understand a vision of yourself that is not shaped by the architecture of patriarchy that has kept us confined for too long. We aren't about to return all taboo to dust, but there are cracks forming and connecting, and eventually we will break down the walls that have kept us trapped. This book was written to inspire new pathways of thought, questions and ideas that break through and help us engage with our inner critics in ways we never thought possible. Whether it be about

Taboo

sex, money, politics, your body, motherhood, marriage, work or beyond, let's begin with radical honesty. The first step to breaking down a taboo is simple and terrifying: I want you to have one conversation that you thought you never would.

acknowledgements

Writing two books in 18 months is only possible when you have a brilliant support network. The following people are the reason I feel safe to write vulnerably.

To the team at Affirm Press – specifically my editor Liz and publisher Kelly – thank you for again guiding me through the creation of a piece of work I truly wanted to put out into the world.

I want to thank my dad. To permit your child to write such personal things about you is generous. My dad is the reason I am charismatic, hardworking and believe that I am capable of anything. He is a father who continues to work hard not to be like his own father. My dad's commitment to always continuing to have the conversation is why I believe change is always possible. I look forward to arguing with him forever. We continue to learn from each other.

Next, my inner circle. Lilli and Annie thank you for supporting me through some dark days on the keyboard.

Thank you to Claudia and Kalila, my forever friends, who I can bounce any creative or business idea off and be met with a podcast-length voice note response that is always just right. Sarah, thank you for week in, week out doing the news with me and all the life stuff off mic too. Thank you to Ruby, Liv and Ash for the *Good Weekend* quiz and NYTimes games when things are looking dire. And thank you to Karolina and Michael, for always having an open door and an opinion much wiser than my natural instinct.

To my mum, my brother and my sister who love me through all my eldest child insanity. Thank you for always allowing me to lean on you, even though I pretend it is exclusively the other way around.

Finally, to Coen. The partner who tells me when I get it wrong, the person who has hard conversations better than anyone I've ever met and the man who drives home at 3am most weeks just to spend a few extra hours with me. I can do everything myself, but I enjoy doing it with you.

references

Alderton, Dolly, *Good Material*, Penguin Press, 7 November 2023

Alderton, Dolly, *Everything I know About Love*, Penguin Press, 19 February 2019

Andrews, Crystal, 'The Pursuit of Beauty: A High Price for Faux-Empowerment', *Zee Feed*, 31 January 2023, zeefeed.com.au/cost-of-beauty-essay/

Australian Human Rights Commission, 'The gender gap in retirement savings', humanrights.gov.au/our-work/gender-gap-retirement-savings

Baker, Nick, 'Middle-aged men are among the loneliest in Australia. What could help to change that?', Australian Broadcasting Corporation, 14 July 2023, abc.net.au/news/2023-07-14/middle-aged-men-experiencing-high-level-loneliness/102563492

Baxter, Jennifer, 'Employment of men and women across the life course', Australian Institute of Family Studies, May 2023, aifs.gov.au/research/facts-and-figures/employment-men-and-women-across-life-course

Beddington, Emma, '"It feels unconditional": the secrets of lifelong friendships – according to lifelong friends', *The Guardian*, 8 March 2023, theguardian.com/lifeandstyle/2023/mar/08/it-feels-unconditional-the-secrets-of-lifelong-friendships-according-to-lifelong-friends

Cain, Sian, 'Women are happier without children or a spouse, says happiness expert', *The Guardian*, 25 May 2019, theguardian.com/lifeandstyle/2019/may/25/women-happier-without-children-or-a-spouse-happiness-expert

Chambers, Clare, *Intact: A Defence of the Unmodified Body*, Penguin Press, 24 February 2022

Contos, Chanel, 'Sexual choking is now so common that many young people don't think it even requires consent. That's a problem', *The Guardian*, 8 December 2022, theguardian.com/commentisfree/2022/dec/08/ sexual-choking-is-now-so-common-that-many-young-people-dont-think-it-even-requires-consent-thats-a-problem

Cohen, Danielle, 'Bumble's Anti-Celibacy Campaign Is Not Going Over Well', *The Cut*, 14 May 2024, thecut.com/article/the-controversy-around-bumbles-anti-celibacy-billboards.html

Cohen, Rachel M., 'How millennials learned to dread motherhood', *Vox*, 4 December 2023, vox.com/features/23979357/millennials-motherhood-dread-parenting-birthrate-women-policy

Contos, Chanel, *Consent Laid Bare: Sex, Entitlement & the Distortion of Desire*, Pan Macmillan, 12 September 2023

Davey, Melissa, 'The four priorities for tackling medical misogyny in Australia', *The Guardian*, 18 December 2022, theguardian.com/australia-news/2022/dec/18/ the-four-priorities-for-tackling-medical-misogyny-in-australia

Davis, Allison P., 'Adorable Little Detonators: Our friendship survived bad dates, illness, marriage, fights. Why can't it survive your baby?', *The Cut*, 11 September 2023, thecut.com/article/adult-friendships-vs-kids.html

Deloitte, '2024 Gen Z and Millennial Survey: Living and working with purpose in a transforming world', 15 May 2024, deloitte.com/global/en/issues/work/content/ genz-millennialsurvey.html

Dolan, Paul, *Happy Ever After: Escaping the Myth of the Perfect Life*, Hay Festival, 25 May 2019

Dublin City University Institute of Education, 'New research shows how TikTok and YouTube Shorts are bombarding users with misogynist content', 17 April 2024, www.dcu.ie/humanities-and-social-sciences/news/2024/apr/new-research-shows-how-tiktok-and-youtube-shorts-are

Dunbar, Robin, '10-Minute Talks: The nature of friendship', The British Academy, 7 April 2021, thebritishacademy.ac.uk/podcasts/10-minute-talks-nature-of-friendship/

Federici, Silvia, *Wages Against Housework*, Autonomedia, 1974

Healthy Male, 'Loneliness: The silent epidemic', 12 September 2022, healthymale. org.au/health-article/loneliness-silent-epidemic

Hill, Sarah, *How the Pill Changes Everything: Your Brain on Birth Control*, Avery, 9 October 2019

References

hooks, bell, *all about love: new visions*, Harper Collins, 22 December 1999

Hopfensitz, Astrid, '"Pretty Privilege": attractive people considered more trustworthy, research confirms', *The Conversation*, 11 April 2024, theconversation.com/pretty-privilege-attractive-people-considered-more-trustworthy-research-confirms-226778

Ipsos and The Global Institute of Women's Leadership, 'One in five Australians thinks women who say they were abused often make up or exaggerate claims of abuse or rape – the highest of any western nation', 4 March 2022, ipsos.com/en-au/one-five-australians-thinks-women-who-say-they-were-abused-often-make-or-exaggerate-claims-abuse-or

Jgln, Katie, 'Why Women Pay the Price for Caring for and Understanding Men', Substack: *The Noösphere*, 13 April 2024, thenoosphere.substack.com/p/why-women-pay-the-price-for-caring

Jones, Daisy, 'If You Grew Up With Money, Stop Being Weird About It', *Refinery29* Australia, 3 October 2023, refinery29.com/en-au/growing-up-with-money

Klein, Naomi, *Doppelganger*, Penguin Press, 7 September 2023

Laan, Ellen, 'In Pursuit of Pleasure: A Biopsychosocial Perspective on Sexual Pleasure and Gender', 27 September 2021, ncbi.nlm.nih.gov/pmc/articles/PMC10903695

La Trobe University, 'National Survey of Australian Secondary Students and Sexual Health', 21 December 2022, latrobe.edu.au/news/articles/2022/release/survey-reveals-teens-attitudes-to-sexual-health

LEGO Group, 'Girls as Young as Five Are Having Their Creativity Impacted by Pressure of Perfection and Language Bias', 5 March 2024, lego.com/en-us/aboutus/news/2024/february/lego-play-unstoppable?locale=en-us

Longstaff, Simon, 'Barbie and what it means to be human', The Ethics Centre, 7 August 2023, ethics.org.au/barbie-and-what-it-means-to-be-human/

Lunn, Natasha, *Conversations on Love*, Penguin Press, 17 May 2022

Marsh, Sarah, '"Kardashian children are sharing skincare routines": experts on gen Z's ageing fixation', *The Guardian*, 20 April 2024, theguardian.com/society/2024/apr/20/young-people-skincare-gen-z-ageing-fixation

Mintz, Laurie, 'The orgasm gap and why women climax less than men', *The Conversation*, 15 August 2023, theconversation.com/the-orgasm-gap-and-why-women-climax-less-than-men-208614

Morgan Stanley, 'Rise of the SHEconomy', 23 September 2019, morganstanley.com/ideas/womens-impact-on-the-economy

Osborne, Tegan, 'Tweens, teens developing complex skincare routines as "Sephora kids" trends on TikTok', Australian Broadcasting Corporation, 21 February 2024, abc.net.au/news/2024-02-21/sephora-kids-should-tweens-teens-use-adult-skincare-products/103488660

Owen, Jesse, Galena K. Rhoades, and Scott M. Stanley, 'Sliding versus Deciding in Relationships: Associations with Relationship Quality, Commitment, and Infidelity', National Library of Medicine, 28 April 2013, ncbi.nlm.nih.gov/pmc/articles/PMC3656416/

Oxfam International, 'Richest 1% bag nearly twice as much wealth as the rest of the world put together over the past two years', 16 January 2023, oxfam.org/en/press-releases/richest-1-bag-nearly-twice-much-wealth-rest-world-put-together-over-past-two-years

Pan X, Hsiao V, Nau DS, Gelfand MJ, 'Explaining the evolution of gossip', *PNAS* USA, 20 February 2024, https://www.pnas.org/doi/abs/10.1073/pnas.2214160121, 121(9)

Perez, Caroline Criado, *Invisible Women: Exposing Data bias in a World Designed for Men*, Penguin Press, 7 March 2019

Perry, Louise, *The Case Against the Sexual Revolution*, Polity, 16 May 2022

Pinsker, Joe, 'Why So Many Americans Don't Talk About Money: The taboos vary by class, job, and circumstance', *The Atlantic*, 2 March 2020, theatlantic.com/family/archive/2020/03/americans-dont-talk-about-money-taboo/607273/

Pitkin, Eliza, 'Laura Bates on the #MeToo backlash: 'The idea that men are the victims now is nonsense', *Big Issue*, 6 July 2022, bigissue.com/news/social-justice/laura-bates-on-metoo-backlash-and-institutional-reform

Plank, Liz, 'can a feminist get botox?', Substack: *Airplane Mode*, 15 March 2024, lizplank.substack.com/p/can-a-feminist-get-botox

Porter, Alice, 'Gossiping Isn't Frivolous Or Immoral — I Love It', *Refinery29*, 23 August 2022, refinery29.com/en-au/gossip-friendship-celebrity-power-accountability

Rowland, Katherine, 'We're sedating women with self-care: how we became obsessed with wellness', *The Guardian*, 1 November 2023, theguardian.com/wellness/2023/nov/01/wellness-industry-healthcare-women-stress

Rushton, Gina, *The Most Important Job In The World*, Pan Macmillan Australia, 29 March 2022

Sussman, Anna Louie, 'A World Without Men: The women of South Korea's 4B movement aren't fighting the patriarchy — they're leaving it behind entirely',

References

The Cut, 8 March 2023, thecut.com/2023/03/4b-movement-feminism-south-korea.html

The Imperfects, 'Dr Emily – Who Do You Desire?', 6 November 2023, https://omny.fm/shows/the-imperfects/dr-emily-who-do-you-desire

The University of South Australia, 'Social media and low self-compassion behind rise in cosmetic surgery', 25 September 2023, unisa.edu.au/media-centre/Releases/2023/social-media-and-low-self-compassion-behind-rise-in-cosmetic-surgery/

Tran, Alvin et al., 'Dating app use and unhealthy weight control behaviors among a sample of U.S. adults: a cross-sectional study', National Library of Medicine, 31 May 2019, ncbi.nlm.nih.gov/pmc/articles/PMC6543621/

Tu, Jessie, '70 per cent of Aussie women experience gender bias while accessing healthcare', Women's Agenda, 13 March 2024, womensagenda.com.au/latest/70-per-cent-of-aussie-women-experience-gender-bias-while-accessing-healthcare/

UNICEF, 'What is female genital mutilation?', unicef.org/protection/female-genital-mutilation

Whiting, Kate, '6 conditions that highlight the women's health gap', World Economic Forum, 15 August 2024, weforum.org/agenda/2024/05/womens-health-gap-healthcare/

Williams, Zoe, 'The orgasm gap – and how to close it: "Don't equate sex and penetration"', *The Guardian*, 21 March 2023, theguardian.com/lifeandstyle/2023/mar/21/the-orgasm-gap-and-how-to-close-it-dont-equate-sex-and-penetration

Wolf, Naomi, *The Beauty Myth*, Penguin Press, 1993

Xerri, Rachael, '"Financial Feminist" explains how the patriarchy is coming between you and your wallet – and what you can do about it', Audible, 21 December 2022

Yaseen, Renee, 'Why are Gen Zers valuing friendships over romance?', *The Washington Post*, 21 September 2023, washingtonpost.com/opinions/2023/09/21/postgrad-relationship-hierarchy-friendships-romance

Please enjoy the first chapter of Hannah's bestselling debut *Bite Back* ...

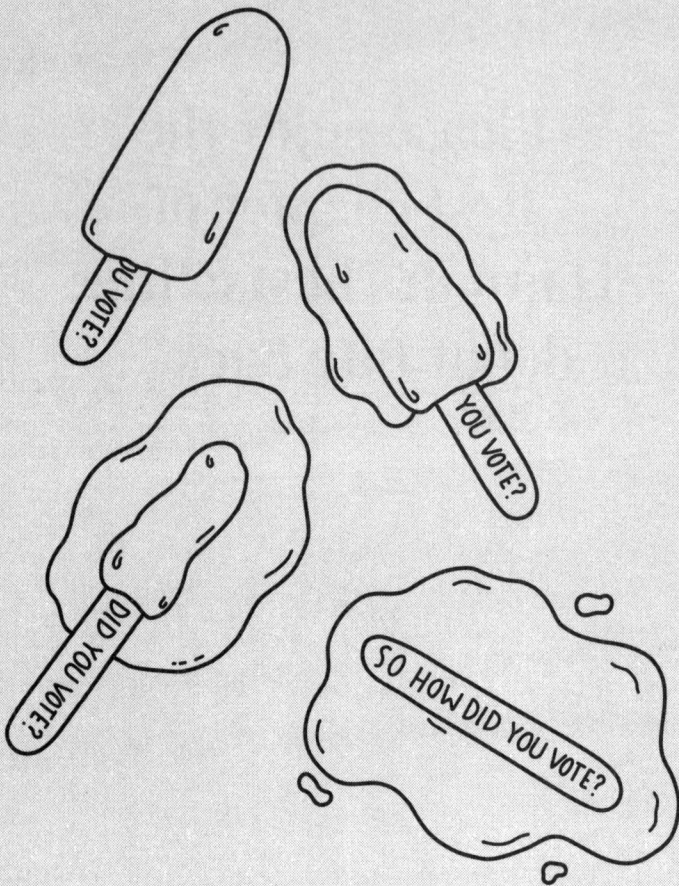

CHAPTER 1

No Politics
Before Dessert

How can we have difficult
conversations with loved ones?

What is the cost of learning? What is the ultimate burden of seeing things from a new perspective, of unwrapping your experiences? What does it feel like to hold them up to the light with wide eyes and renewed insight? What does it take to fuck it up, to admit failure or to change your views? It takes courage. It requires humility. It is challenging to declare liability, to sit with discomfort and to acknowledge responsibility. Anyone can toy with empty words of apology, but to stop sweeping lies under the now six-foot-high rug and start dealing with our shit, reflecting on our conditioning and coming to the table with compassion is a burden not many are willing to carry.

For some women of my mother's and grandmother's generations, acknowledging that girls weren't 'asking for it' with the clothes they were wearing may allow a renewed insight into their own victimhood, and the sexual violence perpetrated against them throughout their life, which was not at all their fault. Unfortunately, it can be easier for some women to shame other women. They end up perpetuating patriarchal views rather than coming to terms with their experience: a lifetime of subjugation at the hands of men. While they may think making victim-blaming comments to the next generation is protective, it in fact engulfs young people in the same lie that disempowers truth-telling, which shifts blame and imposes shame.

This goes beyond feminist issues. For example, does your uncle really hate unions? Or are his views the product of decades of anti-worker messaging and stereotyping perpetuated by both his high-risk workplace and several successive Coalition governments? What would a renewed understanding of his workplace rights mean for the overtime he worked without pay, the work he undertook without the proper safety equipment and the countless breaks and leave he didn't take due to pressure from management? The potential future compensation he signed away in a final deed of release that he didn't have the legal resources to get advice on?

Or take your neighbour who doesn't believe in climate change. It may not be that he's some whacky conspiracy theorist, it may just be that the prospect of total climate annihilation is too terrifying, and denial makes it easier to answer emails and pack kids' lunches and do one million mundane tasks, rather than facing the prospect of a dying planet.

This is not to excuse misinformation, disinformation or the deep offence some of these views perpetrate, but to understand that meaningful conversations with those who oppose us start with understanding the power and influence of their context. Our upbringing, our education and the vast range of life experiences we each carry directly impact our relationship with politics, the news and social issues. Instead of attacking someone for an uninformed view, what if we tried to understand why they have taken up their position? I think, quite often, we can get it. Apathy is light, ignorance seems weightless. We can understand that it is much easier for people to simply detach from discomfort and to become numb to a world filled with so much pain.

Systems of power feed on this disengagement, prioritising tabloids and often exploiting popular culture content as a mechanism of distraction. Our political landscapes, our legal systems and our concentrated media ask very little of those who are agreeable. They comfort them with falsehoods and only ask for their silence in return. Those of us who are working at it every single day, who are engaging and fatigued and struggling to keep up, can empathise with this, because we know that reality is exhausting, relentless and deeply painful. It is difficult to be wrong, and to pursue change, because the truth is a lot harder to stomach. This is where true conversation and understanding begins, with empathy.

Australia does quite a few things poorly, from media diversity to our selection of national holidays, but one of our worst characteristics is our inability to engage in debate, to have difficult conversations that involve healthy conflict. Whether it be the 'Pauline Hanson says what we are all thinking' remark from Grandma while you are slicing Primo Cabanossi together and stacking cubed cheese onto the nibblies platter on Jesus Christ's birthday, or stumbling upon a classic Andrew Bolt headline in your Sunday morning that reads, 'Why do elderly Australian men keep getting jail for raping young boys?', the discussions out there tell me clearly that we have lost the ability to converse with respect, understanding and basic human decency. The birth of the internet, and the inflammatory, divisive journalism fuelled in Australia by Rupert Murdoch's News Corp have driven us to an extreme divide. These mastheads have negated the existence of a political spectrum, instead positioning every issue as a false binary: two polarising viewpoints that are committed to misunderstanding each other, to engaging in harmful debate that ignores the substance and benefits of the respective positions and the nuance, caveats and complexities of any given issue. We are obsessed with labels, with clickbait and with surface-level understanding of every issue, much of which is to be expected in a relentless news cycle that has left each and every one of us fatigued, and this is even after Alan Jones has been stripped of his airtime and relevance.

The internet was idealised as the great democratiser, freeing information from the shackles of journalism's elite and opening the world to new visions, perspectives and commentary from those with lived experiences outside of our own. Instead, we are more polarised and fatigued than ever. We discover that our bodily autonomy and human rights are being taken away via an aesthetic infographic on Instagram, many people depend on the satire of the *Betoota Advocate* as their primary news source, and your friend who tells you they were 'reading an article the other day' is more likely referring to a TikTok video or a Reddit subthread than a high-quality piece of journalism published by a reputable source. Our news feeds and our algorithms are black holes where engagement with complex topics and learning goes to die. As screen time rises, mental health plummets. When we have every

When we consider our own relationship with the news, often there are particular stories or issues that we find too complicated or painful to engage with.

HOW EASY IS IT TO DISENGAGE FROM THE UNCOMFORTABLE, AND *shut out* THE THINGS WE FEEL UNABLE TO COMPREHEND OR TAKE ACTION ON?

answer at our fingertips, we are suddenly paralysed and unable to engage with any topic in a meaningful way.

We are not considering the impact on our psyche of a tiny screen in the palm of our hand that shows us footage of an ongoing war in Ukraine, followed directly by an image questioning the ethics of Botox in feminist discourse, then a post from a guy you went on three dates with in 2018 who just got engaged, rounded out with an inspirational one-line quote posing as genuine therapy advice and a way to make your burger three hundred calories less by taking everything enjoyable out of it in the name of fatphobia, which has been rebranded as wellness culture.

Social media has limited our ability to engage substantially with any given topic. More than three sentences and a topic goes in the 'too hard' basket, in favour of an Instagram reel of a small child discovering the word 'fuck'. Our apathy is born out of feeling overwhelmed and it is completely understandable. Echo chambers are largely the result of algorithms. They are not our own doing but part of a business model in a capitalist society that feeds on our time and shortening attention spans. Put simply, we've really fucked it. 'It' being the climate, our media landscape, that guy from Tinder in the khakis holding a fish whose best line is '6'2" because apparently that matters', the price of a medium oat mocha, the justice system, social media as a tool for change and not a mechanism to perform our entire lives for strangers, fundamental human rights and the empowerment of marginalised communities, just to name a few.

The simple truth is, we are all navigating this world without a clue. We believe that the people we look up to, our heroes, are immune to the problems we have. The blueprint for relationships and families is changing, and many are engaged in a model of revolving-door dating without meaningful connection. Sex remains as taboo as ever at a time when we are so deficient in conversation and consent education. We perform for social media, because if we showcase a happy life to others maybe we will believe it ourselves. We make ourselves palatable, or do not speak at all out of fear of being wrong, instead of having the hard conversation. We are being raised in a world that remains unprepared for the next five years, let alone fifty. We live in a nation and culture divided by a fear of being wrong, not by politics. Large portions of the nation have lost the ability to converse with respect, many commentators and observers no longer recognise and value expertise and instead there is an obsession with being right, with protecting egos in lieu of engaging in meaningful conversation.

Are we supposed to engage in robust conversation with inflammatory racists who are committed to neglecting the basic rights of marginalised people? What is the point of calling out Grandpa Ron at Christmas lunch if I am going to end up as red in the face as Jimmy Barnes during the final chorus of 'Working Class Man' and get absolutely nowhere? What concessions should we give to those who grew up in a different time from us, if any? These are all fair questions and, just a heads-up, I do not have all the answers.

The question we most often ask of ourselves in this space is if we can have friendships and relationships with our family members that simply do not involve politics. I am not here to dictate the dynamics of your relationships or advise you to set quotas for how long you have to spend quizzing your best mate on how often Bob Katter reckons a person in North Queensland is torn to pieces by a crocodile. However, I think two things are important to note. Firstly, if you hold strong political views and you happen to discover this friend or relative has vastly different opinions from you, just like the sudden onset of a haemorrhoid, once you know about it, you'll struggle to forget that it is there. In fact, to drag that horrifying analogy on, if you ignore it, it'll probably just get bigger. Secondly, your ability to disengage from loved ones about politics is an indicator of immense privilege. In 2023, the personal is political. We live in a society where the existence and basic rights of many are not only politicised but also debated on a global stage to further the narratives of 'culture wars'. If your identity is not being used as a political football, you have it pretty good. That privilege might release you from having to think and speak about the heavy. But what if we instead took this privilege as an opportunity to talk about complex social issues and wield this power for good? Your mum, your mate and your colleague are more likely to open their ears to you, and that is a great reason to step in and be brave. When it comes to difficult conversations with loved ones, we should stand up for ourselves and our beliefs, but we should also be advocating for those who are not present, who have less privilege and who experience interlocking marginalisations.

We should not aim to only retain friendships and relationships with people who are directly aligned with us. That is the definition of an echo chamber. However, I also feel the hot rush of vomit in my throat whenever I see a dating-app profile that identifies as 'not political' or 'conservative'. We can refuse to have intimate relationships with people who believe they sit above or outside of politics, and I do not want to spend quality time with people who fundamentally oppose my worldview. But healthy relationships aren't defined by the ability of both parties to be exclusively interested in the same things or to agree: arguing is normal, disagreeing is healthy. It all comes down to the how. How are we communicating our feelings? How are we expressing our opinions? Our needs? Our expectations? Our views? How are we listening to each other and how are we altering our behaviour and views when these challenges are presented? An apology without changed behaviour is meaningless. The silent treatment can be employed as both a protest behaviour and a form of emotional abuse. Conflict is normal, healthy and a central part of humanity. But who are you in conflict? Who do you become in heated debate? What triggers and escalates you? Before we dive into how to have conversations, this is the first interrogation we should be undertaking. If we want to have healthy, expansive conversations, we need to model them from our end first.

For me, I know all too well how awful I am at conducting myself with grace and consideration in these moments of tense discussion, especially when they challenge my values. I arc up and I lash out. I become highly defensive. I cry. I have played games and given the silent treatment. I shut down and withdraw when voices are raised. I find it much easier to see myself as the victim than to sit with discomfort, to hold guilt and to make change. I make assumptions without asking questions. I often fail to understand the experience from another person's perspective. I am argumentative and can be incredibly inflammatory. I have been nasty, manipulative and said things I do not mean with the intention to wound. I have engaged in almost every behaviour that young Hannah watched my parents partake in, the behaviours I always promised little me I would never engage in. My worst experiences, interactions and relationships taught me the most about the person I am, and also the person I want to be. This is not me validating any form of abuse as constructive or necessary to my own growth but identifying that I have tried to reframe these bad experiences from childhood and adulthood as opportunities to sharpen my conversational and conflict-resolution tools. These personal reflections have been valuable insights for me as a writer, an observer and a critic. My self-serving victim mentality will not get me anywhere, and I need to work through these thoughts before I approach someone I want to debate.

One of my grandparents loves nothing more than uploading photographs of physical newspaper headlines to one of their seven Facebook accounts with lengthy commentary designed to stir the pot. They just enjoy the simple pleasure of being controversial and they'll happily tell you so themselves. In fact, it will be disgustingly ego-affirming for them that their years of baiting the more left-leaning members of our family (me) have landed them in this book. Congratulations, anonymous grandparent, you earned it. Especially with that absolute pearler about women not deserving equal rights.

For a long time, the way I explained my conservative grandparents to others was that they had simply run out of software updates. For many of us, this is an easy way to shift difficult and onerous conversation away from ourselves, alleviating guilt about remaining silent and detaching when a slur is thrown just as the pudding is being dished out by the women, probably. All too often, the figureheads of many families are allowed to wave their bigot flag loudly and proudly at every Christmas dinner, birthday lunch and would-someone-please-take-that-bow-off-that-baby's-head baptism, with virtually no repercussions. I can hear my mother, the peacekeeper, whisper in my ear the most disturbing words of comfort, 'Just remember, they'll be dead one day,' as she moves my glass of shiraz out of reach to ensure I won't fire up my PowerPoint presentation on why Grace Tame didn't have to smile at Scott Morrison, which exclusively occurs after glass three.

The 'respect your elders' upbringing most of us endured is the perfect antidote to accountability. We have been trained since birth to perceive age as a currency of power, which demands respect while concurrently remaining immune to consequence and challenge. While it is one thing to acknowledge the lived

WE ARE ALL DEEPLY *flawed,* AND OUR HUMANNESS APPEARS AT ITS MOST RAW WHEN IN CONFLICT. IT IS IMPORTANT TO REFLECT ON HOW WE CAN BECOME BETTER COMMUNICATORS.

experiences of those around us, it is another to allow this claim
to curtail criticism in any form. I hope my future grandchildren
absolutely shit on me for not acknowledging the bodily autonomy
of a bedazzled cushion and I hope I am at least open to hearing
their presentation on the right of a sea cucumber to engage in a
consensual relationship with a strawberry thickshake. Lukewarm
jokes aside, when we aren't listening to and learning from the
young people around us, we are failing.

One of the most harmful elements of Australian culture is
our blind loyalty. I am not talking about your ongoing support of
a sporting team who are wooden-spooners every year, which is
heartwarming. I'm talking about our blind loyalty to political views,
party alignments and friendships. This country has a problematic
relationship with loyalty, and we are more likely to stand by a
person, a team, an organisation or a political party, purely because
we have in the past, than we are to stand by our values and morals
and use them as a platform for connection and conversation. On
the day of the 2010 election, I happily accompanied my parents to
the voting booth after my early-morning netball game. Arriving
with Macca's hotcakes with whipped butter in hand, I loved
watching my parents pick up the how-to-vote cards and read them
carefully at the booth. After some considered selections but with
clearly no prior research to his name, Dad proudly announced
to Mum how he had ordered his ballot. She promptly responded
by informing him that his primary vote had gone to the Labor
candidate. The expression of nausea that overcame his face is
stained in my memory. My father became incensed: 'But I read
the pamphlet. Her policies were *better.*'

The venom in his voice was unmistakable. My lifelong Liberal–National-voting dad's reaction to this discovery is one big, beautiful metaphor for Australians, particularly in our capacity as voters. In this country, many people love nothing more than shitting themselves with fear when they complete the ABC's Vote Compass in the lead-up to an election, lest they discover their values are Greens aligned, while they've been tooting Tony Abbott's horn for the better part of a decade. The rage and shock they feel is laughable. What these individuals are experiencing is either an overwhelming sense of self-betrayal, or that they've been duped by an incredibly intelligent computer program. The reality is, often we simply do not know what we do not know, and most of us would rather stick our heads in the sand for decades than admit to that. This is one of the greatest indictments on our society. When we are presented with a valid, credible challenge to our beliefs and values, it can be such a shock to the system that instead of reflecting on an error and updating our own software accordingly, we double down, riddled with shame. This does not just apply to politics, either. We constantly fail to find nuance, compromise and flexibility in our thinking, instead always pretending to know the reference to that film, that song or that comedian only to spend the rest of the conversation petrified that we will be probed further about said knowledge and exposed in our lie. In reality, we could just admit to not knowing everything that has ever happened and continue the conversation, completely unscathed. Who knows, we might even learn something new. Horrifying.